Peter Gannet was born
midst of the noonday cl
made a dire prophecy tha
and commu

And so he does, when at the age of fourteen he is apprenticed
to a locksmith in Covent Garden. For there in the locksmith's workroom he meets a phantom, stinking of fish, that
beckons him with an empty sleeve. Is it really the ghost of
the last apprentice and, if so, what does it want with him?

Meanwhile, at home in Rotherhithe, Peter's frail twin brother Paul watches his ship in its bottle, one of two made by
the old ship's carpenter, mysteriously being wrecked as
though in a silent, invisible storm.

The Empty Sleeve is a ghost story, a murder story, a story of
fierce envy, a dishonest apprentice and a wall of hands. With
its many-layered plot and powerful, murderous climax, it is a
book that will be read and re-read with the sort of pleasure
that is the true mark of a master storyteller.

Leon Garfield is one of the most highly acclaimed writers of
children's books, having won the first Guardian Award with
Devil-in-the-Fog, the Carnegie Medal (with Edward Blishen)
for *The God Beneath the Sea* (*Smith*, *Black Jack* and *The
Drummer Boy* were all runners-up), and the Whitbread
Award for *John Diamond*. In 1986 *The December Rose* was
shown as a television series, and *Mr Corbett's Ghost* was
filmed for television and cinema. Leon Garfield was born and
educated in Brighton but he now lives in Highgate, a part of
London that has featured in many of his novels.

Other books by Leon Garfield

LEON GARFIELD

THE
EMPTY SLEEVE

Penguin Books

PENGUIN BOOKS

Published by the Penguin Group
27 Wrights Lane, London w8 5tz, England
Viking Penguin Inc., 40 West 23rd Street, New York, New York 10010, USA
Penguin Books Australia Ltd, Ringwood, Victoria, Australia
Penguin Books Canada Ltd, 2801 John Street, Markham, Ontario, Canada l3r 1b4
Penguin Books (NZ) Ltd, 182–190 Wairau Road, Auckland 10, New Zealand

Penguin Books Ltd, Registered Offices: Harmondsworth, Middlesex, England

First published by Viking Kestrel 1988
Published in Penguin Books 1989
1 3 5 7 9 10 8 6 4 2

Made and printed in Great Britain by
Richard Clay Ltd, Bungay, Suffolk

To Gundela and Russell

CHAPTER ONE

vvvvvvvvvv

It takes all sorts to make a world, but only one to unmake it.

On a well-remembered Saturday morning in January, when the air was murderous with wind and snow, like a madman made of feathers, a solitary old man trudged along a street in Rotherhithe, battered, blinded and bewildered by the weather.

The storm was a queer one, and no mistake. It had sprung up out of nowhere; and, in the frightened blinking of the old man's eye, roofs and windows had been sheeted over, church steeples were as stiff and white as dead men's fingers, and he himself was a pauper's Christmas, full of aching bones.

Half an hour before it had begun, he'd seen a woman throw out an old broom. Maybe that had been the cause of it. Soon after, he'd heard a careless boy whistling in the wind. Maybe that had done it. Or maybe it was a sign, a warning of something that was still going to happen. But whatever it was, cause or effect, he'd been rigged and ready. His head was battened down under a greasy cap with leather earflaps, and he was wearing two overcoats and a muffler as long as Methuselah. Like he always said, the ship that sets sail expecting only fair weather is the ship that goes down in the first squall. It was best to be ready for the worst; which was why he'd lived so long. He hunched his shoulders, screwed up his eyes, and tramped on.

His destination, if ever he should reach it, was Gannet's

ship's chandlery on the corner of Hope Sufferance Wharf; and his purpose, if ever he should achieve it, was to buy a pound of half-inch tacks. He was a ship's carpenter who, in his time, had patched up masts and yards and splintered timbers from Zanzibar to the China Seas. But that had been long ago. Now that he was old, he scraped a living by mending chairs and making wooden legs, and carving little ships in bottles, out of old belaying pins and mutton bones.

'Morning, Mr Bagley!'

A snow-blown clergyman crossed his path, waved and hastened into St Mary's Church, pausing under the porch to shake himself out, like a large black dog, before vanishing inside. The old man's eyes glittered with alarm. He reached out to touch the cold iron of the churchyard railings to ward off bad luck. But it was no good. The railings were all bandaged up with snow. Deeply troubled in his spirit, he stumbled across the street and made his way, sometimes sideways, sometimes blundering backwards in his efforts to hide from the wind, until at last he reached the corner of Hope Sufferance Wharf and Gannet's chandlery.

'Shut that door!'

The little shop heaved and rolled, lamps swung, doors slammed, and a pile of invoices, spiked on the counter, fluttered madly as the old man let the weather in, together with himself.

'For God's sake, shut that howling door!'

The dark shop was crowded out with shelterers from the storm, and shadowy faces played hide-and-seek among the hanging boots and jackets, like drowned men slowly dancing under the sea. Obediently the old man shut the door and made his way to the counter, watched by hostile, resentful eyes.

'A pound of half-inch tacks, Mr Gannet,' he croaked,

opening up his overcoats, one after another, in order to get at his money. 'If you'd be so kind.'

'Copper, brass or iron, Mr Bagley?' inquired Mr Gannet, wrinkling up his nose, for the old carpenter smelled and there was no two ways about it, a nasty, cheesy smell that came off him in waves. 'Or some of each?'

'Copper, Mr Gannet,' returned the old man, unwinding a yard of his muffler and wiping his nose on the end of it. 'If you'd be so kind.'

Something was going on. The old man sensed it. Something queer was happening inside the chandlery. As Mr Gannet shovelled the tacks out of a barrel and shook them onto the scales, there was a strange quietness in the shop, and a feeling of secret expectation. Mr Gannet's hands were trembling as he made a brown-paper funnel to hold the tacks; and there was sweat shining on his brow. Shakily he poured the tacks into the funnel; and glanced up at the ceiling, anxiously.

Even as he did so, there was a cry from upstairs, a wild cry like a seagull's scream! Uneasily the old carpenter crossed himself and shoved his money across the counter. He wanted to get out and away, before it was too late. But Mr Gannet took no notice. He was staring up at the ceiling again; and his eyes were as round as port-holes.

'Me parcel –' began the old man, holding out his hand; when, at that very moment, St Mary's clock began to strike the hour.

One by one the heavy chimes banged and echoed in the storm, now loud, now muffled and blown away by the wind. Then, in the midst of the chimes, between the sixth and the seventh – for the clock was striking noon – there came another sound. It was a sound that, although it brought joy and wonderment to all the shop's company, chilled the old carpenter to the bone . . . worse, even, than the winter's wind. It was the tiny spluttering cry and the

3

eerie wailing of a baby that had just been born. The old man shrank into himself and turned as grey as death . . .

A door opened somewhere upstairs. A moment later, eager feet came pattering down and in rushed Mrs Jiffy, the widow lady who lodged aloft and made hats. Her face was shining bright as brass, and she was so full of news that she could hardly get it out.

'Mr Gannet, Mr Gannet!' she panted, 'you'll be needing a signwriter for the shop! From this day on, it's Gannet and S O N!'

Then while Mr Gannet and all the shop's company were taking it in, and getting over it, and thanking God, she went on to tell how Mrs Gannet had come through her labour with flying colours and that the darling new-comer was lusty and well made, with all his fingers, toes and private parts shipshape and Bristol fashion.

'Let's wet the nipper's head!' cried Mr Purvis, of Wines and Spirits, pulling a bottle of rum out of his overcoat pocket. 'Let's see him launched proper on the sea of life!'

'River,' corrected Mr Velonty, the tall schoolmaster, ushering everybody out of the way as Mr Gannet bustled about with cups and glasses. 'The river of life would have been the better expression.'

'To Peter!' cried Mr Gannet, lifting up his glass. 'To Peter Gannet, my son!' Then he downed his drink and hastened upstairs, proud as sixpence, to greet his wife and child.

'Come now, Mr Bagley!' said Mr Velonty, wagging a reproachful finger at the grey-faced old man. 'Be cheerful, sir! Let's have none of your death's-head misery today!'

The old man sighed, and finished off his rum. It was, after all, the right thing to launch a new craft with a splash of something strong; and not for worlds would he have failed to honour the old custom. But nevertheless he was still deeply troubled in his spirit . . .

4

'The clock were chiming,' he muttered. 'And you must know what that means.'

'I do indeed, Mr Bagley,' returned the schoolmaster with a superior smile. 'It means that the clock was in good working order. And nothing more than that!' he added warningly as Mr Gannet came downstairs, all happiness and declaring that the little newcomer was a good 'un all right and well worth taking into stock.

The old man shook his head; but, taking note of the schoolmaster's warning, he held his tongue and kept his dark knowledge to himself. If it hadn't been for the weather, he'd have left the shop then and there; but, as was only to be expected, the wind and snow had got much worse since the coming of the chime-child. So he crept into a corner and heaved himself up onto a barrel, where he sat and peered gloomily at the heedless, happy Rother-hithe folk, the butcher, the baker, the candlestick-maker, the grocer's lady who was old enough to know better, and the spiky-haired fishmonger's lad who wasn't old enough to know anything, all laughing and joking while all the time the unnatural storm was moaning and howling to get in at the birth-room upstairs.

'The last drop, Mr Bagley!' urged Mr Purvis, waving the nearly empty bottle of rum under the old man's nose. 'We'll drink another health!'

He held out his cup. After all, there could be no harm in drinking another health; and, when all was said and done, rum was very comforting when it got down inside.

'To Gannet and Son!' called out Mr Purvis, lifting up his glass. 'A long life and a prosperous voyage!'

'To Gannet and Son!' echoed the shop's company; but before they could drink, there was an interruption. Something else had happened upstairs. There was a groan, a cry, and a sudden shout of women!

'Mr Gannet – oh Mr Gannet!' shrieked Mrs Jiffy, from

the top of the stairs. 'Mr Gannet, oh Mr Gannet!' Then she came down the stairs in a rush and burst into the shop. 'More work for the signwriter! It – it's Gannet and SONS!'

Another one! It was wonderful beyond belief! Nobody had expected him, not Mrs Jiffy, not the midwife, not even Mrs Gannet herself! She'd just cried out, more in surprise than anything else, and there he was! ... like a meek little sunbeam peeping out from the clouds! Such an angel .... every bit as good as the first one ... but, as was only natural, of a smaller, more delicate size ...

'No!' breathed Mr Gannet.

'Yes, yes!' cried Mrs Jiffy; and Mr Gannet, like a man in a dream, went up the stairs for a second time. Mr Purvis produced a second bottle of rum, Mr Velonty said he wasn't surprised and the fishmonger's boy wondered if it was all over and Mrs Gannet had shot her bolt as things generally happened in threes.

Half a minute after, Mr Gannet came back, nodding and laughing in an unbelieving kind of way, and confirming that, upstairs in a cradle made for one, there were now two Gannets, and that he had indeed been blessed with a second good 'un, well worth taking into stock.

Everybody came crowding round, shaking him by the hand and thumping him on the back; and Mr Purvis poured out the rum and proposed the health of the latest who, coming so pat on the heels of a Peter, must surely be a Paul! Up went the glasses and down went the rum, and every face was rosy ... except for one. The old man in the corner, perched on his barrel, like a shabby bird of ill-omen, was grey with dread. He alone knew what he knew; and he alone knew what was needful to be done.

With his ancient heart rattling inside his skinny chest, he eased himself off the barrel and shuffled towards the doorway at the back of the shop. He paused; but as nobody called out, 'Where the devil do you think you're going, Mr Bagley?' he tottered into the dark passageway and began to climb the stairs.

He mounted slowly and painfully, clutching at the bannisters for support. He was a rheumatic old man, and he kept being overcome by waves of weakness and distress. He'd had three, or was it four?, tots of Mr Purvis's rum; and rum, although it gave him boldness, always went straight to his legs. He stopped and waited for a touch of dizziness to pass; then, breathing heavily, he went on to the top of the stairs.

Ahead was a closed door, from behind which he could hear the murmur of women's voices. Then he heard a little coughing cry, followed by the sound of softly chiding laughter. The old man nodded. It was the room. He thrust his hand searchingly into his pocket and tightly clenched his fist.

'It's got to be done . . . it's got to be done!' he mumbled desperately; and he pushed open the door.

The room was bright and hot. The women were by the bed; and, in front of a bloodshot fire, stood a mahogany cradle with brass handles, like a coffin on rockers. Inside it, lying end to end and rolled up tight in swaddling-bands, was the chime-child and his brother. One was smooth and red and full of life; the other was pale and wrinkled and full of death.

The old man trembled. Already he could see vague and fearful shapes twisting and turning in the air above the newborn infants; and the room itself was loose and staggering . . .

'It's got to be done!' he croaked, and, heedless of the shrieks of the amazed women, he drew his fist from his pocket and toppled crazily towards the cradle!

'It's got to be done!' he screeched, as the midwife seized him by the sleeve and Mrs Jiffy caught hold of him by the muffler and half-strangled him as she jerked him off his feet!

'It's got to be done – it's got to be done!' he sobbed and moaned as Mr Gannet and half the shop's company, who'd rushed up the stairs to see what had happened, dragged him out of the room and down the stairs and back into the shop.

'It were salt!' he mumbled wretchedly, as everybody glared down as him like he'd done a murder. 'Look, look!'

He opened his fist and displayed a few filthy grains in the palm of his hand. 'It's salt,' he croaked despairingly. 'It's the only thing that would have saved 'em. Salt in the cradle. It ought to have been done. Twins is bad enough. They'll only have half a soul a-piece. But Saturday makes it worse. Saturday's child will see ghosts. But him what's born on the chime is worst of all. He's the one what'll have communications with the devil. The chime-child, God help him! There ought to have been salt in the cradle . . . there ought to have been salt!'

They threw him out. With one accord, the shop's company turned on the smelly old prophet of doom and bundled him out into the weather. Mercifully, though it was more than he deserved, the storm had blown itself out. The wind had died, the snow had stopped, and a watery sun stared down on a quiet white world, like a sick man's eye on his coverlet.

The old ship's carpenter trudged away, pursued by anger and disgust, and, from the spiky-haired fishmonger's boy, language you wouldn't have used to a dog. His head was bowed, his shoulders were hunched, and his feet made little black graves in the snow.

'There ought to have been salt,' he confided to his muffler. 'There ought to have been salt . . . for the ship that sets sail expecting only fair weather is the ship that goes down in the first squall. And it'll come . . . it's got to come.'

CHAPTER TWO

GANNET & SONS. God Almıghty, what a mess! Mr Wilks, the signwriter, squinted up at his time-battered handiwork, and sighed. The GANNET wasn't too bad, but the SONS was horrible: all flaking and blistered, like Joan of Arc, poor soul! He hoped that the deterioration of SONS in no wise reflected real life.

He glanced up at the morning sky, and shivered. It was a dirty, lumpish grey, like stale porridge. He'd best get a move on before the weather came down on top of him. He set up his ladder, and, with paint-pot, brushes and pommelled stick, he mounted up and set to work to restore the ravages of time.

After he'd been at it for about half an hour, Mr Gannet came out of the chandlery. For a few moments Mr Gannet stood watching the signwriter, who, in his white overalls, seemed to be clinging to the front of the chandlery like a large dead moth.

'Very nice, Mr Wilks,' he said at length, as SONS began to shine once more. 'Just like new, eh?' He smiled, a little ruefully, and ran his fingers through his thinning, faded hair. 'Pity you can't do the same for me!'

'Come, now, Mr G.!' said Mr Wilks, not bothering to look down as he was having trouble with one of the 'S's. 'You don't look a day older than when I was here last!'

'It's been a long day, Mr Wilks! Fourteen years long!'

'You don't say!' said Mr Wilks, making a sympathetic

clucking noise, as if Mr Gannet had confided a private misfortune, like piles or bankruptcy.

'Yes, fourteen years!' repeated Mr Gannet; and as a confirmation, remarked that, in a few hours' time, his eldest son Peter – him that had been an infant when Mr Wilks had last obliged – would be going out into the world on his apprenticeship.

'You don't say! And what's it to be? Same trade as your good self, Mr G.?'

Mr Gannet shook his head. 'Covent Garden,' he said, somewhat heavily.

'Vegetables, Mr G.?'

'Locks and keys, Mr Wilks,' said Mr Gannet, with a touch of indignation that a son of his should be suspected of going in for cabbages. Then he went on to explain that he had had the great good fortune to get Peter apprenticed to a Mr Woodcock, who was a master locksmith and the brother-in-law of Mr Velonty, no less!

'Lucky lad! It's a good trade, I hear!'

'That's just what we keep telling him, Mr Wilks.'

'Don't he care for it, then?' inquired Mr Wilks, sensing a certain grimness in Mr Gannet's voice.

'He will,' said Mr Gannet, his brow darkening, 'when he gets all that nonsense about going to sea knocked out of his head!'

'Ah well!' sighed Mr Wilks, adding a flourish like the golden wave of a golden ocean underneath S O N S. 'We all have our dreams! But your other lad? What about him?'

Instantly, Mr Gannet's heavy looks lightened, and he smiled, almost radiantly.

'Staying at home,' he said. 'He – he's never been very strong, you know.'

'Sorry to hear it, Mr G.,' murmured Mr Wilks, smoothing out a lump in the final 'S'. 'Must be a disappointment to you and your good lady!'

'Far from it, Mr Wilks!' cried Mr Gannet, suddenly warm in the defence of his youngest. 'Our little Paul is an angel, a real angel! And whatever he might lack in the way of his brother's brute strength, he more than makes up for with sweetness of nature!' He paused and then added, more to himself than to the signwriter, 'It's amazing, how twins can have turned out so different!'

'Chalk and cheese, eh?' suggested Mr Wilks, wiping his brushes and beginning to descend the ladder.

'That's right, chalk and cheese,' said Mr Gannet sourly. 'One's good enough to eat, the other just makes a mess.'

'Don't take it so hard, Mr G.,' said Mr Wilks, stepping off the ladder and rubbing his Midas hands on a rag. 'We're only young once!'

'All the more reason to make a good job of it!' grunted Mr Gannet, and was not much comforted by Mr Wilks's saying that it would all come out in the wash. So far as he was concerned, it would have taken Noah's flood to wipe out the recollection of all the aggravation and distress brought about by his first-born.

'So it's today that he goes, eh, Mr G.?'

'Thank God!'

'Don't say that, Mr G. After all, they're brothers. They're going to miss each other. It's wonderful, the love between –'

He stopped. A violent uproar had broken out from upstairs of the chandlery. It was a banging and roaring and screaming, as if murder was being done. Mr Gannet's brow grew thunderous. With shaking hands he paid Mr Wilks for his work, then rushed into the shop.

'– twins,' finished up Mr Wilks. He gazed up at the howling, shrieking chandlery, shook his head and departed, with his ladder cocked over his shoulder, like bad luck on the move.

*

The cause of the uproar was Peter. It always was. Paul had caught him trying to steal an article of his property. He'd actually come into their bedroom just as Peter was stowing it away in his trunk, which was all packed and ready for Covent Garden. Mildly, Paul had protested. Peter had given him a great shove and told him to go and boil his head. Paul had tried again to recover his property, and matters deteriorated sharply. In next to no time, Peter, a loutish, ruffianly boy, was jumping up and down on one of the beds, fending off the screaming attacks of his sickly brother – whose blotchy face was a wet poppy-field of distress – with boot, fist and raucous abuse.

The property in question was a papier mâché carnival mask, made to look like a demon with a savage beak, and gaudily painted red, gold and black. A sailor had brought it into the chandlery just before Christmas, and Paul so longed for it that Mr Gannet, who could deny his youngest son nothing, had bought it for him.

'It's mine – it's mine!' howled Paul, hopelessly trying to snatch the mask away. 'Father gave it to *me*!'

'What do you want it for? You're ugly enough without it!'

'But it's mine – it's mine!'

'It's mine – it's mine!' jeered Peter, in his brother's squeaky voice. 'Everything's yours, isn't it!'

Paul made another rush. He clawed at his beloved mask with all the fierce desperation of a frightened cat. Effortlessly, Peter caught him in the chest with his knee; and Paul went down on the floor with a horrible gasp, like an expiring balloon. Peter laughed; and as he did so, Mr Gannet came into the room.

Mr Gannet was breathing heavily from having rushed up the stairs. He saw his youngest son lying prostrate on the floor. He glared furiously at his eldest. Peter got down off the bed. He grinned stupidly.

'What have you been up to, you little ruffian?' demanded

Mr Gannet.

'Paul fell over,' answered Peter, a boy of few words and most of them bad.

Mr Gannet turned to his youngest, who was struggling to his feet.

'What happened, Paul, dear?' he asked, in a softened voice. 'At least I'll get the truth from you.'

Paul looked unhappily at Peter, and then back to his father.

'We – we were only playing, Father,' he mumbled. He glanced at Peter again, quickly and shyly, as if to say, Please let me save you! A spasm of anger crossed Peter's face.

'He's a liar!' he burst out to his father. 'I got hold of his mask and he went for me like an – an animal!'

Mr Gannet looked hard at Peter, who was holding out the mask. He compressed his lips and, for Paul's sake not wanting to pursue the matter further, contented himself with, 'Give it back to your brother this instant.' Peter did as he was told. 'I'm ashamed of you, Peter,' he said. 'And on your last day, too.'

'Thank God!' muttered Peter, under his breath, but not quite far enough.

Mr Gannet heard him and instantly fetched him such a stinging clout round the ear that his head would have sung with Hallelujahs, had he been that way inclined.

'Never let me hear you speak like that again!' shouted Mr Gannet. 'Now! Shake hands with your brother and let that be an end of it!'

Paul held out his hand. Peter took it, and did his best to crush it into a pulp. Paul bit his lip to stop himself from crying out. Then, when their father had left the room, he murmured, 'I – I'm sorry, Peter.'

Peter stared at him.

'I hate you, Paul,' he said.

CHAPTER THREE

vwvwvwvwvw

Mrs Jiffy had baked a cake for Peter's going away. It looked very like one of her hats. And tasted like it, too.

'Never mind!' comforted Mr Purvis, cutting short Mrs Jiffy's apologies. 'This'll wash it down!'

The old boozer, who'd promised to take Peter to Covent Garden in his delivery cart, had brought a couple of bottles to drink the lad's health (as if the little hooligan didn't have enough of it already!); and poor Mrs Jiffy, almost in tears, pattered off to fetch some glasses.

It was nearly half-past eleven, and everybody was in the parlour, an important little room with a great deal of polished brass and gleaming mahogany that had come Mr Gannet's way in his dealings with the breaker's yard. In fact, as Mr Purvis once said, there was practically everything in it that you needed to go to sea with, save water and a good stretch of sail.

The twins were sitting side by side on an oaken settle (reputed to have come off the *Royal George*), and Mr Gannet was keeping a sharp eye on them. He didn't want any more trouble.

'Now that's a queer thing!' exclaimed Mr Purvis, glancing out of the window. 'It's coming on to snow again!'

'Snow in January,' observed that excellent man, Mr Velonty, who was standing in front of the fire and gently flapping the tails of his dusty black coat, 'is by no means queer, or, to put it better, unusual, in the Northern

Hemisphere between the latitudes of –' He stopped; and, whipping a finger from behind his back, aimed it like a pistol at his two young pupils. 'The latitudes of –?'

'Forty-nine and fifty-five, sir!' answered Paul, without a moment's hesitation; while the lout next to him gave a stupid grin. The boy was as thick as a post . . .

'I meant,' explained Mr Purvis, when everybody had finished congratulating Paul, 'that it snowed on that Saturday when the boys first came into the chandlery, and now, on the very Saturday morning when one of them's going out of it, it's snowing again. And you can't deny that that's queer!'

Mr Velonty smiled; but before he could pour scorn on Mr Purvis's trying to turn a commonplace of weather into a prophecy, Mrs Jiffy came back into the parlour, all tray and elbows.

'I've brought some glasses for the boys!' she cried breathlessly, setting the tray down on a table. 'I do hope it's all right, Mrs Gannet, but I thought that, seeing as how it's Peter's last day, a drop of port wine wouldn't . . . wouldn't . . .'

She trailed away into a papery silence as Mrs Gannet began to express doubts about her sons being old enough to drink spirits.

'Stuff and nonsense, ma'am!' cried Mr Purvis (of Purvis and Nobody, for he'd never married and had sons of his own to add to his sign). 'Why, when I was half their age I was taking my tipple like a man!'

Then, without more ado, he filled all the glasses and handed them round.

'To Peter Gannet! A long life and a prosperous voyage!'

Mr Gannet started. They were the very words that had been heard downstairs in the shop, fourteen years ago! It seemed like yesterday; and, for a moment, it was as if all past time was jumbled up in a huge untidy bag called –

Yesterday. Mr Gannet sighed and drank. He turned towards the window and, with a vague thrill of uneasiness for which he couldn't account, watched the snow come drifting down, thin and quiet, like the ghost of the famous old storm – of yesterday.

Abruptly his thoughts were scattered. The shop bell had jumped and tinkled. A customer. He took a pace towards the door; but for once, Peter was ahead of him.

'I'll go, Pa!' he almost shouted. 'After all,' he added, unkindly mimicking Mrs Jiffy, 'it is my last day!'

Then he was gone, slamming the parlour door and thunderously clattering down the stairs. A lout –

'His last day!' murmured Mrs Gannet, suddenly overcome by sentiment. 'Our little Peter's last day!' while Mr Gannet, recollecting that he'd clouted Peter that very morning for uttering the self-same words, only just stopped himself saying, 'Thank God!'

The customer. An ancient man with a greasy cap, a filthy muffler and a cheesy smell, leaning up against the counter like a slug on a doorstep.

'Ah!' croaked the customer, with a squint of withered cunning, as Peter inserted himself behind the counter. 'You'll be Peter, Mr G.'s first-born. Am I right?'

Peter stopped; partly out of surprise, and partly on account of the old man's stink. He nodded.

'Thought so,' said the customer. 'You was always well timbered, right from the first. Now the other one, Paul, he were chapel-eyed.' The old man looked momentarily anxious. 'He's still afloat, is he?'

'Upstairs,' said Peter, with no great enthusiasm.

'Thought so,' croaked the customer again. 'When I see'd the sign new painted I knew he was still afloat.'

'Do you want to see him?'

'Nar, nar!' said the customer. 'You're the one.'

'Me?' wondered Peter, honestly surprised to be chosen above his brother. 'You sure you got the right one?'

'You're the chime-child, ain't you?'

'Am I?'

The old man shook his frowsy head in shocked disbelief, and made a clucking noise. 'Didn't they tell you, young Peter? You got a right to know. It's your birthright.'

'I never thought I had any rights in this house,' grunted Peter, rolling his eyes expressively upwards.

'That's no way to talk, young Peter,' said the old man reproachfully. 'But never you worry, it'll come, it'll come.'

'What do you mean?' asked Peter, with a little shiver of eagerness at the prospect of something valuable coming his way. 'What'll come?'

The customer looked extraordinarily secretive. Then he beckoned; and Peter, helplessly wrinkling his nose, drew near.

'Tell us, young Peter,' murmured the old man, 'have you – have you see'd anything *transparent*, yet?'

Peter scratched his head.

'Do you mean, like a window?'

'Nar, nar!' grunted the old man. 'More like a – a *person*.'

Peter thought; then shook his head. The old man looked a little disappointed, then he beckoned again. Peter, holding his breath, advanced till he was close enough to see the ghosts of long-dead dinners in the old man's muffler.

'Then tell us this, young Peter,' inquired the customer, with a beady look around the shop that turned the hanging oilskins into crafty eavesdroppers, 'have you ever see'd anything – out o' the corner of your eye, maybe – with *'orns?*'

Peter thought again.

'Do you mean, like a cow?'

'Nar, nar! More like a – a *Imp*.'

'No. Nothing like that.'

'Ah well!' sighed the customer. 'It's early days yet.' He beckoned again, as if inviting Peter to creep inside his coat. 'But it'll come, sure enough,' he croaked. 'Stands to reason. There weren't no salt in your cradle, y'see.'

'Weren't there?' wondered Peter, not knowing whether to be sorry or glad over the lack of seasoning. Like arithmetic, the customer totally mystified him. He was a very queer customer indeed. What did he want? But before Peter could ask, the parlour door opened and Mr Gannet's voice shouted down:

'What the devil are you doing down there, Peter?'

'Customer, Pa,' began Peter; when the old man broke in.

'It's me, Mr G.!' he bellowed. 'Mr Bagley! I come in for that pound of half-inch tacks what I left behind that Saturday morning when the twins was born! Copper, if you'll be so kind!'

There was silence in the parlour. Then Mr Gannet, who'd seen neither hide nor hair of the old ship's carpenter since the unpleasantness of his departure from the shop long ago, said, 'Good God! I thought he'd gone out with the tide years ago! He must be as old as sin!'

'But not so popular, eh?' said Mr Purvis, and heaved with laughter; but Mrs Gannet shuddered as she remembered the shock she'd had when Mr Bagley had burst so wildly into the birth-room.

'Horrible old man!' she whispered; and Mrs Jiffy nodded and said, 'Wicked, wicked.'

'Who is he?' asked Paul.

'Nobody you want to know, dear,' said Mrs Gannet; and Mrs Jiffy said, 'A wicked, wicked old man.'

'Why? What's he done?'

'He's only an old ship's carpenter,' explained Mr Velonty, who felt that altogether too much was being made of Mr Bagley. 'A very foolish, superstitious old man.'

'I'd better go downstairs,' said Mr Gannet abruptly, 'before he starts filling Peter's head with his nonsense!'

'And on his last day, too!' said Mrs Jiffy, as Mr Gannet hurried from the room, leaving the door open in his haste to get down to the shop.

'What are you doing, Paul, dear?' asked Mrs Gannet.

'I was going to shut the door, Mother,' Paul replied; and did so, but remained standing close beside it.

Old Bagley. Filthy old devil! Looked just the same as always. Most likely he'd never even crawled out of his clothes in all of the fourteen years!

'It's been a long time, Mr Bagley,' said Mr Gannet, and tried to control his anger when he saw that the old man and Peter looked as thick as thieves. He wondered how much of Mr Bagley's rubbish had already got inside Peter's thick head.

'You can go upstairs, Peter,' he said curtly. 'I'll attend to Mr Bagley.' Peter was about to go, when, to Mr Gannet's annoyance, the old man laid a hand on the boy's shoulder, and stopped him.

'Your lad here's been telling me that he's off on his apprenticeship today,' said Mr Bagley. Mr Gannet nodded. The old man looked sombre. 'Bad luck to begin a voyage on a Saturday,' he said.

Mr Gannet lost his temper. 'Really, Mr Bagley –' he began; when the old carpenter completely took the wind out of Mr Gannet's sails by saying that he was glad to have caught Peter at home as, it's being nigh on the twins' birthday, he'd brung 'em something a-piece.

'That – that's very good of you, Mr Bagley,' said Mr Gannet awkwardly; and watched the old man fumble in the bulging pockets of his filthy coat. God knew what undesirable and evil-smelling articles were about to be produced! Even Peter, Mr Gannet was glad to see, was watching the old man's antics somewhat glassily ...

'Here they are, Mr G.,' he grunted at length, dragging out two green glass bottles and laying them on the counter. 'I'd have brung 'em sooner, only they wasn't dry.'

Mr Gannet stared. His mouth fell open. So did Peter's; and father's and son's heads converged over the old man's gifts. Inside the bottles were two little white sailing ships. They were, so far as Mr Gannet could see, perfect in every detail, right down to the tiny hatches and delicately scored planking along the decks. They were marvels of workmanship. The old man must have strained his eyes over them for years.

'I made 'em out of mutton bones,' said Mr Bagley proudly. 'And I rigged 'em with Air.'

'Air?'

'Air,' repeated Mr Bagley, and, lifting an earflap, pulled out a frowsy lock to make his meaning clear. 'Air. Horse's Air.'

Mr Gannet nodded wonderingly, and peered closely at the spider-fine shrouds and the little poop lanterns that were no bigger than a flea's thumbnail.

'Zanzibar and the China Seas,' mumbled Mr Bagley, blinking away the recollection of an ancient sea-fret. 'That were their run, Mr G.' Then he went on to explain that he'd built the two vessels adjacent and that there wasn't so much as a coat of varnish to choose between them. Saving for their names, of course. One was called '*Peter*, out of Hope Sufferance Wharf', and the other was *Paul*, out of likewise. He pointed to the engraving across the sterns. Mr Gannet took his word for it, as the writing was too small to be read without spectacles.

'Give a ship a name and you give it a soul,' said Mr

Bagley solemnly. 'And that ain't all.' He beckoned his listeners still closer. 'Them two bottles,' he breathed, 'are the very ones the twins' health was drunk out of, on the day they were born. I carried 'em off with me. So now you can see, Mr G., that there's a shade more'n just a smidgeon of souls aboard.'

Mr Gannet drew back. He disliked the old man's childish magic more than he could say. He hoped there'd be no more of it. He glanced at Peter. There was a look of stupid greed on the boy's face, and his hand was twitching to get hold of his ship.

'I done the best I could for your boys, Mr G.,' confided the old man, earnestly. 'I rigged their vessels under tops'ls only. That way, they'll ride out the squalls.'

Mr Gannet's heart sank. He guessed what was coming; and sure enough, the old fool trotted out his weird rigmarole of the ship setting sail expecting only fair weather being the ship that went down in the first squall.

'It's best to be prepared for the worst, Mr G., for them squalls has got to come. Most of all, for young Peter here. Saturday's child, born on the chime, will surely see ghosts and have communications with the devil.'

There! It was out! Damn the old wretch!

'And – and will it be the same for Paul, Mr Bagley?' whispered Peter, staring with awe at the two ships.

'Nar, nar. He'll be the watcher. He'll be the crow in the crow's nest.'

The shop bell jumped and tinkled again, and everybody in the parlour breathed a sigh of relief. The old man had gone. A moment later, there was the sound of footsteps mounting the stairs. Paul opened the door and Mr Gannet, followed by his first-born, came in, confirming that the customer had been old Bagley all right and not his ghost.

'Horrible old man!' shivered Mrs Gannet.

Mr Gannet looked uncomfortable and said that the old man meant well and that he'd been good enough to bring presents for the boys.

'Give Paul his ship,' he said to Peter, who was holding his hands behind his back in a manner that instantly had aroused Mr Velonty's schoolmasterly suspicions. Silently, Peter produced one of the bottles. Instantly there were cries of amazement and admiration. Paul approached, and Peter handed him his ship.

'Are you sure that's the right one?' demanded Mr Gannet.

'Yes, Pa. I kept it in my left hand.'

'His *left* hand. Typical!' muttered Mr Gannet. 'Oh well, I suppose we should be thankful he knows his right from his left.'

Peter looked as if he was going to say something, but Mrs Gannet hurriedly said it was getting late and time for Peter to go and make himself ready.

'Let's have a look at that ship of yours,' said Mr Purvis, as Peter was half-way out of the door; then, as the boy hesitated, he added. 'Don't worry! I'll be careful with it.'

Silently Peter handed over Mr Bagley's marvellous present, and left the parlour to go upstairs. Mr Purvis carried the bottle to the window and examined it carefully. He shook his head and sighed.

'Extraordinary, when you think of it! A smelly old man, not worth tuppence, can turn a shabby bit of mutton bone into something really beautiful ... something that anybody would be proud to have on his mantelpiece!'

He sighed again, and Paul asked if he, too, could look at Peter's ship. Mr Purvis passed it to him.

'Be careful with it, Paul,' said Mr Gannet anxiously.

'I will, Father.'

'And don't mix it up with yours.'

22

'I won't, Father.' He smiled almost mischievously and murmured, 'I'll keep it in my *right* hand.'

Everybody laughed and Paul, seating himself on the settle, held the ships side by side. Then he put them down beside him to admire them from a different view. Then, hearing Peter coming down the stairs again, he picked them up with a curious twisting movement, almost as if he had crossed his hands.

'My ship! Where's my ship?' demanded the overcoated and mufflered Peter, clumping into the room.

Mutely, Paul held out one of the bottles.

'Your right hand, Paul,' smiled Mr Velonty. 'Remember, it was in your right hand.'

Paul looked confused. He went red in patches. 'Oh yes,' he said; and gave Peter the other ship.

For a moment, it looked as if there was going to be another quarrel between the boys; but it passed and everybody went downstairs to see Peter safely onto Mr Purvis's cart. Then came last-minute farewells, last-minute tears, and last-minute advice to the departing son.

'Work hard, Peter, work hard!' called out Mr Gannet as the cart began to move.

'Be good, dear, be good!' wailed Mrs Gannet, waving a damp handkerchief at the huddled figure in the back of the cart, sitting on a trunk boldly labelled in white paint: *Peter Gannet. Care of S. Woodcock. Master Locksmith. Cucumber Alley. Covent Garden.*

'Ah well!' thought Peter, brooding over his curious birthright. 'Ghosts and the devil. Hm! Better than nothing, I s'pose!' Then he looked down at the ship he was clutching in his lap. He smiled. 'All aboard the Zanzibar and the China Seas!'

The wind blew, the snow fell faster, and the rattling of the cart wheels over the cobbles sounded like thunder.

*

Paul had gone upstairs to his room.

'Do you think he's all right?' Mrs Gannet murmured.

'I'll go and see,' said Mr Gannet. 'Most likely he's only having a little cry.'

But Paul was not crying. He was sitting on his bed, staring hard at Mr Bagley's gift.

'That's a fine ship you've got there,' said Mr Gannet gently, and laid a hand on Paul's shoulder. Paul looked up. He seemed almost frightened. 'Can I look at it?' Mr Gannet asked. Paul shook his head violently, and clutched the ship to his chest. Mr Gannet sighed, and left the boy alone.

When his father had gone, Paul put the ship on the floor and, for several minutes, remained crouching over it, like a watchful crow. Then he got up and put the ship on top of a chest of drawers. As he did so, he caught sight of his face in a mirror. He gave a little groan, and turned away.

'I hate you, Paul!' he whispered.

CHAPTER FOUR

vwvwvwvwvw

Saturday night; very late. Cucumber Alley, fifty yards of high-class shops between Queen Street and Great Earl Street, was quiet and empty; and the iron gates at either end were locked and bolted, to keep out the midnight murderers, wandering beggars, and thieves. Half-way down, on the western side, next door to the Bible shop and opposite Temmick and Stint, the jeweller's, stood the premises of S. Woodcock. You couldn't miss it. There was a huge iron key hanging outside, grinning in its teeth, as if it had just finished locking up a boy.

The locksmith's shop was as black as hell. A wind that had come from nowhere had blown out Peter Gannet's candle as he lay in the narrow apprentice's bed behind the counter in the shop. It was the first time in his life that he'd been alone in the dark; and he did not like it. As he lay, stiff as a corpse, helplessly listening to the creaking and groaning of the horrible old house, he felt by turn terrified, miserable and hungry; and his face was wet with tears.

Contrary to popular opinion, Peter Gannet was not as thick as a post. He had feelings, like everybody else; and his feelings had been deeply, unjustly hurt. He had been got rid of, and he knew it. He had been squeezed out, like a blackhead; and all because, instead of a human brother, he'd been cursed with a holy little saint. All his life, since first he'd been able to stand up without holding on, he'd

25

been blamed for having every natural advantage; he'd been shouted at and pushed aside, while sick-faced little Paul had been treasured up like he'd been God's own waistcoat button.

'Damn you, damn you, damn you!' he whispered, as he thought of all the godly folk back at Hope Sufferance Wharf who'd smashed his dreams, blasted his hopes, and at last condemned him to the iron gaol of S. Woodcock. The 'S', he'd found out, stood for Samuel; but he could have supplied something more suitable that began with the same letter.

Mr Woodcock was a long, grim gent with a jaw like a padlock that he only seemed to open to put food in; and his sarcastical cow of a wife was worse. She was the sister of that loud-mouthed, ear-twisting bastard, Mr Velonty; and she had her brother's face so exactly that you wondered if they took it in turns.

'At Mr Woodcock's table,' she'd said to him with a wormy little smile, just as he'd started to spoon up his soup at dinner, 'we say grace before meals. Even if we are a boy quite without any, Master Gannet.'

He'd grinned, like he always did when he hadn't immediately understood what was said to him; but then, when he'd worked it out, he'd felt like he was going to be sick.

He sweated and clenched his fists at the hateful recollection, and swore to himself that Cucumber Alley, which had only just seen the first of Peter Gannet, would, as soon as he could lay his hands on enough money, be seeing the last of him. He would be off like a phantom in the night, for the docks and a ship, and Zanzibar and the China Seas.

His old dream of going to sea, far from having been knocked out of his head, had just been hammered in and counter-sunk by the locksmith and his wife. But he needed money. He remembered what had happened when he'd tried before, in Hope Sufferance Wharf. He'd asked the burly mates and bo'suns – men with arms like ropes and faces like angry maps – who'd come into the shop on business, if they wanted a cabin-boy, a fingers-to-the-bone working cabin-boy? One and all they'd said, like a pain in the arse, lad! And if ever they was to catch him trying to sneak aboard without paying his passage, they'd flay the hide right off of him and return it, pickled in brine, to his pa. Oh yes! he needed money all right!

His thoughts drifted to the only thing he possessed that was of any value: Mr Bagley's present, the little white ship in the green glass bottle. He wondered how much it would fetch and where he might sell it? He reached out into the chilly dark to make sure it was still on the floor beside him. He touched it. The glass felt strangely warm, almost as if there was life in it. He shivered as he remembered what the old man had said, about a smidgeon of his soul being inside the bottle.

There was no doubt that Mr Bagley, ancient and smelly though he was, had made a deep impression on him. Particularly with his weird prophecy. He couldn't get it out of his mind; and now, as he lay in the chilly blackness of the locksmith's shop, it was almost as if Mr Bagley was in the dark, right next to him, and croaking in his ear:

'Saturday's child, born on the chime, will surely see ghosts and have communications with the devil . . .'

His heart began to beat unevenly; and in a confused kind of way – for he was dazed from his efforts to get to sleep – he tried to work out how he might get money from the devil without selling his soul. Then, with a jerk of excitement, he remembered that the old man had rigged his soul so that it was ready to weather the squalls! So it was all right! All he needed was the devil . . .

Suddenly he sat up. His tiredness left him. Somebody was coming. He'd heard footsteps creaking secretly down the stairs. A moment later, huge shadows loomed as a wobbling flame, cupped in a cautious hand, came swaying down into the shop.

'Are you awake?'

'Yes.'

'Thought so. Didn't s'pose you'd get much sleep on your first night.'

It wasn't the devil; it was Polly, the Woodcocks' kitchen girl, with a coat over her nightgown and big, bare, bony feet. She put her tin candlestick on the counter and began to rustle in the pocket of her coat.

'Seeing as how you didn't eat hardly enough at dinner to keep a bird alive,' she whispered, producing something wrapped up in newspaper, 'I fetched you some bread and dripping.'

He stared at her in bewilderment; then, gratefully, he reached up and took the parcel.

'Not so much noise!' she breathed as he began to unwrap it. 'You'll wake the family!' She leaned over the counter until her wispy hair floated dangerously close to the candle and there was a smell of singeing. 'They got ears as sharp as knives!'

She wasn't what you'd call a beauty. Even though her heart was in the right place, nothing much else was; and there was something about her gleaming nose and anxiously open mouth that reminded Peter of a china jug back home . . .

'That's right,' she murmured as he began to eat. 'Feed the inner boy. Got to keep body and soul together, y'know.' She watched with satisfaction as he munched away. 'Now don't you go leaving no crumbs. Brings in the rats and mice, and we don't keep no cat in the house . . . *saving Miss Maria, of course*!' she added under her breath, and then looked round as if she wondered who could have said such a thing.

'What about Miss Maria?' asked Peter, recollecting the Woodcocks' grown-up daughter who'd sat opposite him all through dinner and had looked at him like he'd been an unpleasant smell.

'Miss Maria?' repeated Polly with a puzzled frown. 'I never said nothing about Miss Maria! The very idea! Why, I'd sooner have me tongue cut out than I'd speak disrespectful of Miss Maria Woodcock! Or of her ma. And the same goes for the master, too!' she said defiantly; and then added, again under her breath, *'Poor soul!'*

'Why did you say that?'

'Say what?'

'Poor soul.'

'I never did! You must be imagining things. Maybe it's because you're sleeping the wrong way round. The other one always used to sleep with his head to the window.'

He asked her again about the poor soul, thinking that there must be more to the locksmith than he'd supposed; but she looked as blank as a wall, and went on about the other one who'd always slept with his head to the window. He was the last apprentice, Thomas Kite. He'd been gone about a month, somewhere up north, Polly thought, after having unexpectedly come into money. He was quite the gent, was our Thomas Kite . . .

Unexpected money. That was queer. Polly's words had chimed in exactly with his own thoughts! Of course, it was only a coincidence; but, for a moment, he couldn't help wondering. Then, just as he was about to dismiss it from his mind, there came another coincidence; and it was so striking that it made him jump.

'Caught a flea?' inquired Polly, sympathetically.

He didn't answer. He was staring at the newspaper. He'd just picked up the last piece of bread and dripping when an item of shipping news, heavily stained with grease, had caught his eye. 'Sailing this day from Tilbury,' he read, 'for Cape Town, Zanzibar and the China Seas, the *Gannet*. 900 tons. Saloon Accommodation available at Twenty Pounds.'

He could hardly believe it. There he was, Gannet, sailing for Zanzibar and the China Seas! Of course it was an old paper, and that Gannet was, most likely, half-way round the world by now; but soon there'd be another one. All he needed was twenty pounds . . .

'What are you looking at?' asked Polly, trying to peer over his shoulder.

'Look!' he said, holding up the paper. 'It's me, Gannet!'

She looked; then she shook her head. 'You want your eyes seen to,' she said. 'It's *Garnet*, not Gannet, dear.'

He could have cried.

'Did you want to go to sea, then?' murmured Polly, seeing the bitter disappointment in his face. He nodded. 'Never mind,' she said kindly. 'I 'spect there's many a sailor out there in the cold and wet what dreamed of being a locksmith's apprentice when he was little. So count your blessings, dear, on all your fingers and toes!'

All his fingers and toes. Ten of each. Twice ten were twenty. Thanks to Mr Velonty, he knew that much. Twenty blessings . . . if only the Devil would turn them into pounds! Suddenly he looked up.

'What's that?' he muttered.

'What's what?'

'Listen!'

A curious jingling noise had started up. It was very faint but quite distinct. It seemed to be coming from behind the locked workroom door. Polly frowned.

'There you go again,' she said. 'Imagining things. I can't hear nothing. Must be your empty stummick making you light-headed. You finish up your bread and dripping and you won't go hearing things God never meant you to!'

He stared at her; then he looked at the workroom door.

Instantly the jingling stopped, and the door seemed to stare back at him blankly, as if it was saying, like Polly, 'You must be imagining things.' Maybe he was. Maybe the jingling had been inside his head ... Obediently he finished up his bread and dripping.

'Give us the newspaper,' whispered Polly, when the last mouthful had gone down, 'and then nobody'll be any the wiser about tonight.'

He gave it to her. She glanced at it, muttered, 'Gannet, indeed!' then folded it up and stowed it away in her pocket. 'Not a word, mind!' she said, raising a warning finger. 'In a locksmith's house things has to be kept locked up. And that means everything: spoons, jools, *and* tongues!'

Then, with a nod of satisfaction at having fed the inner boy with nourishment and good advice, she lighted his candle from her own, and went away.

He listened as her big bare feet creaked up and up the stairs until, at last, the noise of them dwindled away into the general creaking of the house.

'She was wrong,' he muttered angrily. 'It *was* Gannet!'

He stared up at the weird shadows on the ceiling and walls, and tried to make sense of them. On a sudden impulse, he shifted the candle and, clasping his hands together and poking up two fingers for horns, he made a shadow devil on the ceiling, to bring him luck.

Then, suddenly, he heard the jingling noise again. It was louder than before and sounded like the clinking of glasses, or even the jingling of money. He listened carefully and fancied, although he could not be absolutely sure, that he could hear a faint murmur of voices. He felt very frightened and wondered if thieves could have got into the workroom. He sat bolt-upright and stared at the door. Instantly the jingling sound stopped, just as it had done before; and the door, with its polished brass keyhole plate, stared back at him as if to say, 'You must be imagining things.'

He remained sitting upright and listening for several minutes; but the workroom stayed as quiet as the grave. Then waves of tiredness overcame him. He blew out his candle and went to sleep.

CHAPTER FIVE

vwvwvwvwvw

There was money in keys; and in more ways than just poking them into keyholes. You'd be surprised! Peter Gannet found out in the morning, after church . . .

It was bright and cold; and the Woodcocks, grim and holy in their Sunday worst, were talking with neighbours, while the new apprentice shuffled his feet and waited, a little way off. Weary and aching from his unfamiliar bed, and clutching the prayer-book Mr Velonty had given him and which wouldn't have fetched sixpence, he was thinking despairingly of the devil and twenty pounds.

'I'm Jay,' said a short, powerful-looking Sunday youth, suddenly coming up to him with a hand shoved out like a bunch of asparagus. 'Jay, of Gross and Shirtie's, the staymaker's in the Alley.'

'Pleased to make your acquaintance,' said Peter, taking the offered hand and pumping it up and down two or three times. 'I'm sure.'

'Likewise,' said Jay, plainly impressed by the power of Peter's grip. 'You're the new St Peter, ain't you?'

'You got the name right,' said Peter sourly; 'but not the inclinations.'

Jay grinned; and explained that St Peter was the name given to all locksmith's apprentices, no matter what they was called at home, on account of their being the keepers of the keys. He looked Peter over, shrewdly.

'There's money in keys,' he murmured, tapping the side of his nose. 'You'd be surprised.'

Peter Gannet started. It was extraordinary. For a second time money had been mentioned exactly when he'd been thinking of it. Weirdly he began to feel that the coincidences that were littering his path were, perhaps, more than coincidences . . . He glanced back. The Woodcocks were still talking.

'Nobs,' said Jay, referring to the grand-looking couple that the Woodcocks were presently engaged with. 'Lord and Lady Marriner. Bow Street. Number twenty-seven. Your people won't want you hanging about to queer their pitch.'

Sure enough, Mr Woodcock, catching Peter's eye, gestured to his loutish new apprentice that he should return to the shop on his own.

'Like I was saying,' said Jay, fondly linking his arm with Peter's and beginning to guide him away, 'there's money in keys.'

'What keys?' asked Peter, uneasily wondering about midnight burglary, savage dogs, and ending up hanged.

Jay told him. Mentioning no names, he confided quietly, but there were persons in the Alley, persons of good faith and able to keep their mouths shut, who would be willing to pay out hard cash for a lend of the key to the gates; the gates in question being them cruel iron brutes at either end of the Alley what was locked up at ten o'clock every night.

Now although it was true that every household in the Alley had its own key to the gates, that key was not very easily get-at-able by the aforementioned persons of good faith. Which meant they had to be back in the Alley before ten o'clock. Which meant they was forever cut off from the spiritual refreshment of a good booze-up and whatever titbit of female company might be picked up round

Monmouth Street or Shorts Gardens on the cheap. It was, said Jay, a straight violation of human rights.

'You can say that again!' muttered a second youth, who, almost unnoticed, had fallen in beside them as they walked back to Cucumber Alley. He was tall and thin, with a powdery white complexion and powdery white hands. He looked like a ghost.

'Dawkins,' explained Jay; 'of Peacock and Gravey, the pastrycook's, likewise in the Alley. One of them persons I was telling you of, what can keep their mouths shut.'

'You can say that again,' confirmed Dawkins, and shook Peter by the hand.

'Gannet,' said Peter, 'of Woodcock's. Likewise in the Alley.'

'Ah! The new St Peter! And about time! It's been a month since the last one went.'

'Thomas Kite, wasn't it?' said Peter.

'That's right,' said Dawkins with a frown. 'Crafty little twister. Sell you the silver out of his ma's hair if you didn't watch him.'

Now it was Jay's turn to declare that you could say that again; and went on to explain that Kite had been in the habit of demanding money from three or four apprentices separately for a lend of the key on the same night.

'Gannet knows about the key, then?' inquired Dawkins.

'I was just telling him,' said Jay.

'It's number seventeen,' said Dawkins, 'hanging up on your workroom wall. You can't miss it. It's got a bit of black thread tied round it. Generally you pass it over in The Bedford Head at eight o'clock and it's money on the nail. Then you pick it up again first thing in the morning out of Stint's devil –'

The devil! Peter caught his breath. Once again, words spoken by someone else, by a stranger almost, had chimed in uncannily with his thoughts!

'What's wrong?' asked Jay, curiously. His arm was still linked with Peter's, and he'd felt a sudden jerk.

'Oh, nothing. Just one of them shivers, I expect.'

'Somebody just walked over your grave,' advised Dawkins. 'Leastways, it shows you won't be buried at sea.' He chuckled. 'You should have been a sailor, young Gannet!'

Peter stared. For a moment he had a marvellous sensation of flying. He felt as if he was caught in the grip of a mysterious wind that was whirling him along, and that the sharp coincidences that kept glaring at him as he passed them by were really signposts, shouting out, 'This way!'

'What about the devil?' he muttered, half-afraid that he hadn't heard right.

'Stint's devil,' said Dawkins. 'Ain't you noticed him then?'

Peter shook his head.

'Up there,' said Dawkins, aiming a ghastly finger. 'The gent with the horns and tail.'

They were back in the Alley and almost outside the locksmith's shop. They halted.

'He could do with a lick of paint,' said Jay, gazing up critically at Temmick and Stint, the jeweller's, where, on a ledge above the door, there crouched a little wooden devil, hugging himself with glee. 'If you ask me.'

'His head opens up,' said Dawkins, 'on a hinge. And there's a hole inside, very convenient for the key.'

It was impossible not to feel a sense of shock and angry disappointment. The devil in Cucumber Alley, although undeniably a devil, was a ridiculous, shabby little fellow, no more than two feet high. The paint was flaking off his scarlet jacket, the gold was coming off his horns; and the worm had got into his tail. He was a mockery of Mr Bagley's prophecy, and an insult to Peter's dreams. Yet there was something about him, chiefly about the uncomfortably knowing malevolence of his grin, that made Peter falter and think again; and wonder if Stint's ugly little devil was really the tip of something huge and dark that was lurking below, like the unseen immensity of an iceberg . . .

'It's shocking,' said Jay, reproachfully, 'to have let him get into that state! Gives all of us on The Sin a bad name.' Then, seeing the look of curiosity on the new apprentice's face, he explained that, what with Stint's devil being set up opposite the Society for the Propagation of Christian Knowledge, what sold Bibles and plaster saints of neither sex, the two sides of Cucumber Alley had become known as Godside and The Sin.

'We're on The Sin,' said Dawkins. 'Jay and me.'

'But we're all really on The Sin,' said Jay, comfortingly; 'no matter where we lays our heads. After all, we're only young once.'

'Thank God!' muttered Peter, from the bottom of his heart; and Dawkins said, 'You can say that again!'

Then Jay took the opportunity to remind Peter that there was money in keys, and as much as sixpence had been known to change hands at The Bedford Head.

'What about Tuesday?' proposed Dawkins.

'Don't rush him,' said Jay. 'Give him time to find his feet.'

'They're at the end of his legs,' said Dawkins, with a touch of irritation. 'If he ain't found them by now, he never will. What about –'

He stopped as Jay lifted a warning finger. The worthy shopkeepers and their wives were beginning to come back into the Alley, with solemn Sunday faces and fearful Sunday hats. Politely Jay raised his cap to his employers as they passed him by.

'You wouldn't think,' he murmured, glancing after them, 'that they was once like us!'

'Then for God's sake,' said Dawkins, 'let's get a move on before us gets like them! What about Friday?'

Peter frowned; not because he was undecided, but because he was trying to work out how long it would take him to get twenty pounds at the rate of sixpence a night. He looked up. Jay and Dawkins smiled encouragingly; and Stint's devil grinned.

CHAPTER SIX

vwvwvwvwvw

Nobody's good or bad; he's only either better or worse than his neighbour. It was Peter Gannet's bad luck to be mostly worse; and in particular, he was worse than the last apprentice, Thomas Kite, *the other one* . . .

'So you're young Gannet. Hm! I can't say as you measures up to the other one,' grunted Mr Shoveller, Woodcock's workman, as he opened up the workroom on the Monday morning, took off his coat, and muffler and put his head through the loops of his apron, like it was a noose, God forbid! 'Now he were a good 'un, and no mistake!'

'He was a crafty little twister who'd sell you the silver out of his ma's hair,' thought Peter angrily. 'You old fool!' But he held his tongue and tried to look respectful. After all, he and Mr Shoveller weren't going to be acquainted for long . . .

It was this desperate hope that kept him alive and lifted his spirits when they were at their lowest, through all the iron days and bitter nights in the locksmith's house. And it was only this hope that stopped him bursting into tears and giving up the ghost when first he stared round the smoke-blackened workroom that was to be his cradle, his nursery and his daily life, where nothing was thought about, talked about, mended or made, but locks and keys, hinges, clasps and bolts.

'Ketching flies, young Gannet?' sarcastically inquired

Mr Shoveller, as Peter's wandering gaze fell upon a vast congregation of keys hanging, like an iron tapestry, from one of the workroom walls, and he stood, stock-still, with his mouth ajar.

There were hundreds and hundreds of them, of all sizes and complication; from surly iron grandfathers of keys, such as might have locked up a whole town, right down to tiny brass grandchildren, mere shiny infants of keys, such as might have locked up a baby or a mouse. Eagerly he looked along the rows for the key that was worth money, number seventeen with the bit of black thread round it, when suddenly he recollected the mysterious jingling he'd heard on the Saturday night. It must have been caused by a wind coming down the chimney and jostling the keys on their nails. Nothing more than that . . .

'The other one,' grunted Mr Shoveller, settling himself down at the bench, 'would have asked what was to be done. He wouldn't have just stood there, like a block of wood, grinning at nothing and waiting to be told!'

He was a stern man, was Mr Shoveller, a man of grunts and shrugs, with little squinting eyes and a nose like an old potato. He was a man of hammers, rasps and files, of screeching iron and sudden flowers of sparks that kept shooting up all round him, like a fiery garden. He had an uncomfortable way of looking up at you sharply, as if through an invisible keyhole, and when you least expected it. But that was his way with everybody, even with Mr Woodcock himself, when the master locksmith came down into the workroom at nine o'clock in the morning to examine the work in hand before going out on business.

'I'm off to Barnard's Inn,' Mr Woodcock would say; and Mr Shoveller would give him a sharp little keyhole squint.

At eleven o'clock, on the very stroke, the old misery

would send Peter to fetch his morning mug of ale from the public-house on the corner of Neal's Yard.

'I see you can jump to it when the fancy takes you, young Gannet,' he'd say, as Peter nipped smartly towards the door. 'Pity it don't take you more often. The other one were smart in all his ways!'

'Slimy little creep!' muttered Peter as he went.

It was always a relief to get out of the grim, dark shop, even for a hasty couple of minutes; and he looked forward to meeting up with other apprentices who were on similar errands. He was interested to discover that they were as anxious to make his acquaintance as had been Jay and Dawkins; for in Cucumber Alley, a St Peter was never in want of friends. There was Crane of the hatter's, and Robbins of the bootmaker's; but it was Jay and Dawkins who were his oldest friends . . .

'Well?' asked Dawkins, on the Wednesday, as they met in the public-house. 'What about Friday?'

'Give him a bit longer,' advised Jay, before Peter could answer. 'After all, what's another couple of days? Don't go rushing him. No sense in spoiling the ship for a ha'porth of tar.'

'Who said anything about ha'pence?' demanded Dawkins impatiently. 'It's sixpence on the nail.' He turned to Peter. 'Have you seen where it is yet?'

Peter nodded. He'd seen the key all right. It was the third one from the end on the top row.

'Friday, then,' said Dawkins. 'After all, you got to make a start sometime, as the sailor said to the virgin. See you at eight o'clock in The Bedford Head.'

He walked back slowly and carefully, carrying Mr Shoveller's mug of ale and thinking deeply, more deeply than he'd ever thought in his life before. Dawkins was right. He had to make a start. It was no good waiting for the devil. No matter what the risk, he'd have to take the first step himself if ever he was to escape the shackles of what his father and Mr Velonty called 'the real world' . . . which, so far as he could see, amounted to exchanging the prison of childhood for the narrow gaol of being grown up.

He paused outside the locksmith's shop and looked up at Stint's devil, half-hoping for a wink or a nod of approval; but before the shabby little fellow could signify, one way or the other, the window above him shot up with a rattle and a bang and out popped Ruby Stint, the jeweller's daughter; or, at least, the top half of her.

She was a fat girl of about fourteen, much given to low-cut dresses, so that she was as much an eyeful as she was a windowful. She smiled down at the good-looking locksmith's apprentice and waved a dumpling hand.

Peter's heart quickened. He liked girls and, to the best of his belief, they liked him. Back home he'd often been told admiringly, by Rotherhithe girls, that he'd a wicked grin and naughty, roving eyes; and even Mrs Jiffy had once declared that, when he grew up, he'd be breaking hearts like new-laid eggs. But until now, he'd never been able to take advantage of his charms, as he'd always been saddled with holy little Paul. He winked and grinned and waved back at the jeweller's daughter.

Then he jumped and spilled a quantity of Mr Shoveller's ale as a hand fell heavily on his shoulder. It was Polly, with a parcel under her arm and a drip on the end of her nose. Instantly, the window above Stint's devil slammed shut.

'*Fat little trollop!*' said Polly, under her breath; and then, with a stern look, announced: 'The master wants you. He's next door, in the Propagation.'

Peter felt panic-stricken. In his experience, when people wanted him, it wasn't for the pleasure of his company. Usually it meant that they'd found out something. Miserably he wondered if, by some unnatural means, his conversations with Jay and Dawkins had come to Mr Woodcock's ears.

'Make haste,' said Polly; and then, poking at her parcel, murmured, 'I saved you an extra bit of pie. Got to keep body and soul together. Got to feed the inner boy, y'know. I'll leave it behind the counter for when you comes back.'

Peter nodded and went into the Bible shop, trembling with apprehension and spilling even more of Mr Shoveller's ale. The dreaded Mr Woodcock was leaning up against a bookshelf with a holy book open in his hand. To Peter's surprise, the locksmith's face looked almost human, as if what he'd been reading had performed the miracle of changing iron into flesh and blood; and there was something about his expression that made Peter suddenly remember Polly's 'the master, *poor soul*!'

'Ah! Gannet!' said Mr Woodcock, looking up and beholding his apprentice shaking in the doorway, like a piece of paper in the wind. 'I've some good news for you!'

Peter tottered with relief; and he wondered wildly what the good news could be. Perhaps they were missing him so much at home that they'd cancelled his apprenticeship? Perhaps somebody had died and left him twenty pounds? Perhaps –

'On Friday night,' said Mr Woodcock kindly, 'Mr Velonty will be coming to dinner. I expect he will be bringing you news of home, Gannet; and, although I know you are not a scholar, you will have time to write a letter to your brother for Mr Velonty to take back with him.'

Good news! Peter Gannet could hardly believe it was possible that the master locksmith honestly thought that Mr Velonty was good news. God alone knew what was in his catalogue of disasters!

'Thank you, Mr Woodcock, sir,' mumbled Peter; and, as he went back to the workroom, he wondered if, perhaps,

Mr Woodcock had been boozing. Come to think of it, he had smelled faintly of something like rose-water and gin.

Mr Shoveller was not pleased. 'The other one,' he grunted, peering into his insufficient mug, 'never spilled a drop.'

Peter shrugged his shoulders, and instantly received one of Mr Shoveller's sharp little keyhole squints. It was plain that Mr Shoveller didn't take kindly to any criticism, spoken or implied, of his angel, the other one.

But Peter wasn't thinking about the other one. He was worrying himself sick about Friday night and whether Mr Velonty's presence would prevent him keeping his appointment at The Bedford Head. He tried to keep his eyes off the wall of keys, and, in particular, off the key with the bit of black thread round it, as Mr Shoveller's continual looks unnerved him and made him feel as if his most private thoughts were being spied on, through a keyhole in his head. Whenever he felt the need creeping over him to look again at the key, he most resolutely fixed his gaze on the opposite wall, the wall with the little barred window, as if it was the most interesting thing he had ever seen . . .

'Ah!' said Mr Shoveller. 'I was wondering when you'd notice. The other one noticed right away. Kept his eyes open, he did.'

What the devil was the old fool talking about? Peter looked at the wall again. It was just a dirty old wall, badly plastered, and with what looked like pale patches of mould coming out all over it, like a disease.

'Hand next Heart,' said Mr Shoveller, getting up from his bench and hobbling over to the wall, with a file in one hand and a half-worked key in the other. 'That's what that is, young Gannet, Hand next Heart. It's an old custom. Goes back, I shouldn't wonder, to when Noah and his carpenter lads made the Ark. See them hands?' he said, jabbing his file at the pallid patches on the wall. 'Them's the hands of workmates what have gone on to better things. Marked up in chalk, they were, on the day they left. That's so that if ever they looks in again, for old time's sake, they can claim their hands off the wall, and it's pie and beer all round!'

Then, as if suddenly overcome by a melancholy feeling for an enormous dead past, he began tracing over the pale smudges with his file. 'There's old Joey Barnett,' he murmured fondly. 'He were a lad all right. Dead an' gone, though, dead an' gone. And that's Tom Pulham, so they say; but he were before my time. Must be dead these fifteen years . . .'

'And – and do they ever come back and claim their hands, Mr Shoveller?' asked Peter, at last seeing that the smudges really were hands, spread-out hands reaching in all directions, like blind men feeling for a door. 'Them that's still alive, that is.'

'If they ain't been shamed by bad workmanship or wrongful practice,' said Mr Shoveller, grimly wagging the half-finished key at the new apprentice. 'Like some I could mention. Now there's a hand for you!' he said, tapping his file against a bunch of dead white fingers that were crawling under the window, like the ghost of a spider. 'It's his. It's the other one's. And, as you can see, young Gannet, it ain't all thumbs; like some I could mention!'

Peter looked at it, and suddenly had a violent desire to hit it with a hammer, or to scrub it right off the wall. It reminded him irresistibly of the good little hand, always so white and delicate, of his brother Paul; and from the bottom of his heart he cursed the bad luck that had sent him from one stinking saint to another. And it didn't help to know that Thomas Kite was a crafty little twister who'd swindled his way down the Alley; so far as Mr Shoveller was concerned, the sun shone out of his arse.

At length, when the day was ending and Mr Shoveller was getting his head out of the noose of his apron, Peter Gannet gave way to his feelings. He edged up to the wall of hands and, with a venomous and secretive jerk, he slapped his own hand against the white one as if he would squash it, like an unwholesome moth. 'There!' he breathed. 'You slimy bastard!'

He jumped back. He took his hand off the wall as if it had been red-hot. He had received a most unpleasant sensation. The hand on the wall had moved. It had answered his pressure, palm for palm, finger for finger.

'You look a bit white around the gills, young Gannet,' said Mr Shoveller, looking at him curiously. 'Bowels, I expect. Take a dose of rhubarb last thing at night. That'll shift 'em.'

He began putting on his coat and Peter, holding his breath, touched the hand again; but this time it was cold and flat and only a chalk mark on a wall. He stared at it. It seemed to stare back as if to say, like so much else in the locksmith's house, 'You must be imagining things.'

CHAPTER SEVEN

vvvvvvvvvvv

There were four keys to the workroom door. Mr
Woodcock had one, Mr Shoveller had one, there was one
hanging up with all the others on the workroom wall; and
there was another that was kept in a drawer in the shop,
which, in turn, was locked and the key hidden behind a
mirror on the first-floor landing, facing you as you came
up the stairs.

In a locksmith's house, Polly had said, things had to be
kept locked up. And most of all, keys. The great congregation of keys that hung on the workroom wall were
the keys to all the locks that Mr Woodcock had made.
They were the heart and conscience of the locksmith's
house, and represented the security of countless unknown
lives. In unlawful hands, God knew what treasure-houses
they could have opened up, and what dark secrets they
could have let out: what pearls and diamonds, what mad
children and what dead wives . . .

At five o'clock on the Friday, Mr Shoveller locked up
the workroom and went home to his lodgings in Cler-
kenwell, leaving the apprentice to mind the shop for the
last hour. At six o'clock – for in the winter months the day
ended early – Mr Woodcock came down, poked about to
see what had been left undone; and told Peter Gannet to
bolt the front door and get himself ready for dinner.

Peter waited till he heard the locksmith shut his door
upstairs and a murmur of voices start up; then he nipped

up to the first-floor landing as noiselessly as a shadow. For an alarming instant, as he fumbled for the key behind the mirror, he was glared at by his own reflection; and was shocked by how young and frightened he looked. Shakily he got hold of the key and crept down the stairs with it. Then he opened the drawer, took out the other key and, in a moment, was inside the workroom.

It was dark; but there was just enough of a glow from the dying coals of the furnace for him to see what he was doing. He climbed up on a stool and, with trembling hands, lifted number seventeen off its nail, stuffed it into his pocket, and climbed down again.

As he did so, he caught sight, out of the corner of his eye, of the wall of hands. He grew cold. The pale hands seemed to be upraised in anger and dismay at the apprentice who was betraying his master's trust. Violently he shook his head. It wasn't like Mr Gannet's first-born to be so fanciful.

He locked up the workroom, replaced the key in the drawer, and took the last key back upstairs. As he moved the mirror, he couldn't avoid seeing his reflection again. This time the watcher in the glass looked ten years older.

Dinner was horrible. That pig, Mr Velonty, sat next to Miss Maria and exactly opposite Peter Gannet, so that his big square face, exactly the same as Mrs Woodcock's only more bluish about the chin, kept getting in the way of the sideboard clock.

'And don't you want to know how your family is, Gannet?' he inquired; and then, without waiting for an answer, turned to Mrs Woodcock and said that he was sorry to say that the boy, unlike his brother, was not a boy of deep feelings. As he moved his head, Peter saw that it was half-past six; then the clock disappeared as Mr Velonty loomed back and told him that everybody at

Hope Sufferance Wharf was in good health and surviving his absence without any ill-effects.

Everybody laughed at Mr Velonty's little joke; and Mr Woodcock said grace, and Mrs Woodcock smiled her wormy little smile and said she was pleased to see that this time Gannet had waited for the blessing before piggishly gobbling up his soup. Mr Velonty nodded approvingly, tucked his napkin under his chin and bent over his plate; and Peter saw it was twenty-five minutes to seven.

He felt hot, unbearably hot. In fact, he was sure he could smell himself scorching. He was sitting with his back to the fire which, in honour of Mr Velonty's visit, had been built up till it was blazing like an oven. Dazedly he wondered how many apprentices the Woodcocks had had, and whether it was their usual practice to cook them when they were new, and serve them up when there was company. Certainly, the mutton chops that Polly had put on the table looked most peculiar and might easily have come off a boy –

'Gannet!' bellowed Mr Velonty suddenly. 'Pay attention! Mr Woodcock is talking to you!'

Peter jumped, caught a glimpse of ten to seven, and wondered fleetingly how long it would take him to get to The Bedford Head . . .

'As I was saying,' said Mr Woodcock, waving his fork in the air, 'give me –' Then he stopped dead. Polly had come in with the gravy.

Everybody waited. It was always like that at the Woodcocks' table. All talk stopped when Polly came into the room; and went on again as if nothing had happened as soon as she'd gone. It was just like she'd told him. Even tongues were locked up in the locksmith's house. You could almost hear the keys turn and the bolts slide home inside the Woodcocks' heads. Then Polly went out and shut the door behind her.

'– an honest boy, Gannet,' said Mr Woodcock, resuming the waving of his fork which had remained stock-still in the air during Polly's visit. 'Give me a trustworthy boy, and I'll make a good locksmith of him. I don't ask for cleverness –'

'– Mr Woodcock knows you are not clever, Gannet,' put in Mr Velonty. 'I have told him,' and everybody at the table nodded as if Mr Velonty had only confirmed what they'd known all along.

'All I ask,' said Mr Woodcock, 'is a boy who can be trusted with locks and keys.' And he pointed his fork straight at the key in Peter's pocket.

'Trusted,' said Mrs Woodcock.

'With keys,' said Miss Maria.

'That's all I ask,' said Mr Woodcock; and lowered the fork that, quite by chance, had just given his apprentice the worst moment in all his life.

He'd nearly fainted. In fact, something of the sort must have happened to him, because the next time he caught sight of the clock, it was nearly ten past seven, and he'd no idea how so much time could have passed without his noticing it.

The key was digging into him painfully. It seemed to be biting him with sharp iron teeth. But he didn't dare to shift it as he was terrified it would slip out of his pocket and fall on the floor with a loud clang. So he sat, in motionless agony, while Mr Woodcock, between mouthfuls, lectured him on the strict rules and stern maxims of the locksmith's trade; and Mrs Woodcock and her daughter kept chiming in at the end of everything, and sometimes in the middle; and the sideboard clock kept playing hide-and-seek with Mr Velonty's head. Half-past seven . . .

'It is not for nothing, Gannet,' said Mr Woodcock, his harsh voice grating monotonously on his apprentice's ear, 'that this shop is on the Godside of Cucumber Alley –'

'– The Godside, Gannet,' said Mrs Woodcock.

'And not on The Sin,' added Miss Maria, smiling one of her mother's wormy little smiles; 'Gannet.' Then she looked, not at Peter, but at her uncle, that swine Mr Velonty, who, ever so slightly, tightened his lips and shrugged his shoulders.

It was a queer moment. There was a quietness following her words, and an odd sensation of people looking the other way. Peter Gannet felt as if he wasn't there; then Mr Velonty coughed meaningly and Mr Woodcock said, 'Yes ... yes ... not on The Sin, Gannet,' as if his mind had wandered and he was trying to pick up the thread of what he'd been saying.

'You know about The Sin, Gannet –'

'The Sin,' said Mrs Woodcock; and Miss Maria said, 'Gannet.'

'I mean Mr Stint's little devil and all that ...'

'The devil,' said Mrs Woodcock.

'And all that,' murmured Miss Maria.

'But of course it's just a word, Gannet,' went on Mr Woodcock, frowning at his plate as if he'd found a worm in his cabbage. 'Mr Stint is quite as good as the rest of us. In fact ... in fact, you might just as well say the devil is as much our paymaster as he is Mr Stint's, with all the costly temptations in his window.' He paused, as if waiting for the usual support from his wife and daughter; but nothing came, so he continued, speaking more quietly and still frowning down at his plate: 'If there was no devil, Gannet, if there was no wickedness in the world, if there was no pride, or envy, or selfishness in our hearts, there would be no need for locksmiths. There would be no need to lock things up and – and to hide them away. There would be no need to –'

'– Oh, for goodness' sake!' interrupted Mrs Woodcock, suddenly losing patience with the way things were going. 'Come down out of the clouds, Mr Woodcock! Just think of what you're saying! Why, if we had no locks on our doors, we'd all be murdered in our beds! Everybody knows that! Really, Mr Woodcock, for a sensible, grown-up man, you do talk –'

She stopped dead as Polly came in with the pudding, put it on the table, and went out.

'– nonsense, you know!' she finished up.

Mr Woodcock didn't say anything and the pudding went down in silence. There was no more talk about locks and keys and honest apprentices, and Peter Gannet felt that the worst was over. He had ridden out his first storm. At five minutes to eight, he asked, nervously, if he might go. Mr Woodcock looked at him sternly.

'The letter,' he said. 'Have you done as I told you and written the letter to your brother for Mr Velonty to take back with him?'

'I – I –' began Peter, when Mr Velonty, who could see through his old pupil like he was a pane of glass, sadly shook his head.

'I don't think we need to hear your excuses, Gannet,' he said; and then, to Mr Woodcock, 'I'm afraid, brother-in-law, that your good advice was thrown away on him. He is not a thoughtful boy, he is not a boy of deep feelings . . .'

Mr Woodcock sighed. 'Very well, Gannet. You can go now.'

Peter stood up. He felt the key slither in his pocket, and prayed that there wasn't a hole in it.

'One moment, Gannet,' said Mr Velonty. 'I have a message for you from your father. He was anxious that you should take good care of the present that Mr Bagley gave you.'

'Yes, sir.'

'It is very delicate, you know. You haven't broken it, I trust?'

'Oh no, sir!'

'You surprise me! I understand that even your brother, who, God alone knows, is more careful than you, has had a small misfortune with his own vessel. One of the sails has come away from its rigging . . .'

It was past eight o'clock before he left the shop. Although he was late, he couldn't go out without first examining his ship. He kept it, with all his other possessions, in a cupboard under the stairs. His hands were shaking as he took it out. He peered at it carefully. The little white ship still sailed on untroubled in its green world. The wind in Cucumber Alley was set fair, no matter what storms there might be raging in Hope Sufferance Wharf.

Gently he replaced his vessel in the cupboard and, with a great sigh of relief, went off to The Bedford Head.

CHAPTER EIGHT

vwvwvwvwvw

He ran all the way. He fairly pelted through the darkly twisting maze of little streets that lay beyond the iron gates of Cucumber Alley. Even so, he was horribly late. It was striking half-past eight when he arrived, dazed and breathless, outside The Bedford Head.

Just before he went in, he glanced quickly up and down the street. He couldn't help it. Ever since he'd left the shop, he'd had an unpleasant feeling that somebody, or something, was lurking behind him, silent and unseen . . . But he saw only strangers –

'Don't be such a fool, Gannet!' he whispered to himself as he pushed open the door. 'You'll be frightened of your own bloody shadow next!'

The Bedford Head was one of those dim, funereal public-houses of quiet nooks and shadowy corners, with discreet cubby-holes shut up inside black wooden walls, like private chapels of rest. Quiet drinkers sat about in heaps and bundles; looked up, saw Gannet, then looked down again. No Jay or Dawkins. A waiter in a dirty apron, carrying a tray, asked him if he'd taken root? He gave a stupid grin, and shuffled out of the way.

He began to feel sick. He was too late. Jay and Dawkins had gone. The stolen key was suddenly huge and heavy in his pocket, and all he could think of was getting it back on the workroom wall. He began to back away towards the door –

'Looking for your friends, young man!'

A gentleman sitting alone in one of the cubby-holes, leaned forward and smiled up at him pleasantly. With a twinge of alarm, Peter thought he recognized him; or at least the face seemed familiar even though he couldn't put a name to it.

'In there,' murmured the gentleman, tapping on the wall of his compartment with a silver-topped cane.

Instantly a head appeared over the top. It was Jay's. It saw the gentleman, turned deferential; then saw Gannet and vanished with a wild and frantic glare. Gannet nearly fainted with relief!

Jay and Dawkins had almost given him up. They were sitting huddled up together, clutching empty glasses. Their nerves were in tatters from leaning out sideways to watch the door, and having to keep jerking back again to avoid the beady eye of the waiter who was turning nasty about their taking up seats and not buying more drinks. Dawkins in particular was in a bad state.

'And about bleeding time!' he muttered savagely, brushing aside young Gannet's passionate excuses. 'I ain't paying out good money for a lend of the key for only half the night! Don't you start coming the Thomas Kite with –'

He stopped as there came another knock on the dividing wall. The three apprentices stared at one another in alarm. Had they been overheard? Then Jay dug Gannet in the ribs and pointed. The silver knob of the gentleman's cane was poking up over the top of the partition, like a thousand-pound Punch and Judy. It was the shape of a lion's head, snarling.

'Was I right, young man?' came the gentleman's voice. 'About your friends, I mean?'

Jay prodded again.

'Yes, sir!' responded Peter quickly. 'It was them, sir! Thank you, sir!'

'*Your lordship!*' hissed Jay. 'Didn't you recognize him? Lord Marriner! Bow Street, number twenty-seven!'

'I mean, your lordship!' corrected Peter anxiously.

The lion's head vanished with a silver snarl and a faint chuckle. Peter stared at his companions. For God's sake, what was to be done? How much had his lordship overheard? Jay shook his head.

'Not to worry,' he breathed in Peter's ear. 'He's a real gent. He don't go listening in to what's none of his business. Breeding, you know. You can always tell. It's in the blood.'

Nevertheless, it was noticeable that Jay and Dawkins never raised their voices above a fly's whisper, even when it didn't matter.

'*The key!*' mouthed Dawkins. 'Have you got the bleeding key!'

'The money!' whispered Peter. 'What about the bleeding money?'

'*Don't shout!*' begged Jay, going into agonies in case his faith in breeding was put to the test.

Peter tapped the side of his nose to show that he understood, and dragged the key out of his pocket. It was a marvel it hadn't rusted away with sweat. He held it out and tried to stop his hand from shaking. Dawkins's eyes gleamed. He produced the money; then he put it away again, double-quick, as the beady-eyed waiter saw it and approached. Unasked, he put down three glasses of ale.

'I didn't –' began Dawkins indignantly, when the waiter said:

'Compliments of next door,' and went away.

'As the waiter said,' came his lordship's voice, before the apprentices had got over the shock. 'With my compliments, boys.'

Jay stood up, went round to the other side of the partition, and thanked his lordship warmly, on behalf of his colleagues and himself.

'Think nothing of it,' returned his lordship. 'I was young once myself.'

Jay came back and settled down.

'What did I tell you?' he murmured, breathing stale fish into Peter's face. 'There's breeding for you! There's blood!'

They raised their glasses and Jay courteously proposed the very good health of their benefactor, to which his lordship responded in kind. They drank. The ale tasted bitter and strong, stronger than Peter was used to; but he needed it . . .

'*The key!*' Dawkins was mouthing at him again. 'Give us the key!' He was holding out the money again. Peter took it and, quick as a ferret, Dawkins snatched the key.

'Got an appointment,' explained Jay. 'That's why he's in such a state. Newman Street. Miss Harrison. Number three, second floor. Been dreaming about her and saving up for her for weeks. Time's money for Dawkins, and money's dreams, and dreams is Miss Harrison –'

'You can say that again!' muttered the pastrycook's apprentice, his thin, plain face transfigured with longing. 'She's got a bosom on her like a pair of cottages loaves! So help me!'

But Jay, the staymaker's apprentice, knew better.

'All wire and whalebone,' he murmured shrewdly. 'Believe you me, Dawkins, there's more flab than flavour in them there hills.'

'I'll tell you tomorrow,' grunted Dawkins, finishing off his drink. 'Anyway, I'd sooner spend all me money on a night in Newman Street than be caged up in Cucumber Alley any more with nothing to go for but that fat lump, Ruby Stint! So help me, I would!'

He stood up and brushed down his coat, which gave off faint clouds of flour.

'Nobody denies,' said Jay, quietly, 'that Miss Harrison is the superior article. It's only right and proper. After all, like it says in the Bible, her price is far above Ruby's; but –'

'– the good things in life, Jay,' said Dawkins, 'ain't never free.' Then, with a whispered promise to young Gannet that he'd remember to leave the key in Stint's devil, he left The Bedford Head like it was on fire.

Jay shook his head. Dawkins, he said, was a very passionate individual. Women ruled his life. He didn't know no moderation. Although it was natural for the blood to flow warm in young veins, he, Jay, wouldn't have been surprised if, in Dawkins's case, it was hot enough to boil an egg.

'But he'll get over it, young Gannet,' he murmured, getting up and laying a fatherly hand on Peter's shoulder. 'He'll burn himself out. Sooner or later it comes to all of us. But until then, there'll always be money in keys.'

With that, the short, powerful-looking staymaker's apprentice, whose trade it was to keep desire alight with wire and whalebone, stumped away. Peter was alone.

He felt much easier in his mind now that the business was done. All his earlier fears, and, in particular, the unpleasant sensation of being followed, had left him. He was all right. His sails were spread and the wind was steady and fair –

Suddenly he started. His neighbour had knocked again.

'All alone, young man?' came his invisible lordship's voice; and round the side of the partition peeped the little silver lion, snarling delicately.

'Y-yes, your lordship. They've only just gone . . . my friends . . . and I was just going to – to –'

He faltered as the silver lion poked round a little further, almost as if it meant to bar his way.

'Waiter!' called out his lordship abruptly. The waiter

hastened to his side. 'Bring me a glass of port. No! Two glasses. One for the young gentleman next door. But a small one, mind! We don't want a tipsy boy on our hands, do we!'

'Thank you, your lordship,' muttered Peter.

'What was that? I can't hear you through the wood. Speak up, boy!'

'I said, thank you, your lordship,' said Peter, relieved that his lordship hadn't been able to hear properly. It was all very well for Jay to talk about breeding, but it was better to be sure. After all, even a lord was only human ...

'You're Mr Woodcock's boy, aren't you?' said his lordship, kindly.

'Y-yes, your lordship.' (He *had* been able to hear!)

'A fine man, Mr Woodcock. You should do well with him.'

He hadn't! Thank God – thank God! The waiter returned with the port.

'Your health, Mr Woodcock's boy!' proposed his lordship.

Peter gulped down his drink in one violent swallow. He wanted to get out of The Bedford Head as quick as he could. Although Lord Marriner was amazingly affable and generous, Peter couldn't help feeling uneasy with him. He half stood up, then sat down again. The silver lion was still barring his way. Most likely it was just lying along the seat and its owner had forgotten about it.

'That's a very beautiful walking-stick, your lordship,' he said, hoping to prompt him into moving it.

'I'm glad you think so, Mr Woodcock's boy,' said his lordship; and Peter had the weirdest feeling that the lion's snarl had turned into a grin. 'I collect them, you know. In fact, Mr Woodcock's boy, I collect a great many beautiful objects; not only silver, but pictures and porcelain and bronze . . . oh, my house is a real museum!' he declared, with a pleasant chuckle in his voice. 'Your master, Mr Woodcock, will know all about it. He and his last apprentice were in my house for weeks, putting in new locks. Why! they practically lived there!'

Peter sighed wearily while his lordship rambled on, describing all his treasures, it seemed, one by one . . .

'But the most beautiful item of all,' his lordship murmured at length, 'the loveliest item in my house is – is Lady Marriner herself!'

He paused, as if he wanted to give full weight to his sudden outburst of gallantry. Peter felt uncomfortable. He didn't know what was expected of him. All he really wanted was to say that he ought to be going; but instead, and to his own surprise, he found himself beginning to talk about the only beautiful item that he himself possessed: his little bone ship in its green glass bottle.

Afterwards he wondered what had made him think of it then. Maybe it was because he felt that Lord Marriner, being a collector, might be interested? Or perhaps it was because the ship, and its strange importance to him, had been at the back of his mind all the time?

'It must be quite valuable,' said his lordship, when Peter had finished describing Mr Bagley's wonderful workmanship as best he could. 'You should take great care of it.'

'I – I was thinking of selling it!' said Peter, before he could stop himself.

'Indeed!' said his lordship. 'I think I should like to see it.'

'I – I was wondering if it was worth – worth twenty pounds!'

At this, his lordship laughed heartily, either at the enormous amount proposed, or else because of the sudden desperation that had come into the young apprentice's voice.

'That's a great deal of money, Mr Woodcock's boy! And I'm not really a collector of ships in bottles! But we'll see, we'll see! You'd better go back to your master now. It's getting late. In the meantime, look after your beautiful ship and perhaps one day – who knows when? – we might be able to do each other a favour!'

The silver lion had gone. Peter understood that he was now free to go. He stood up, his heart thundering with excitement. Lord Marriner would buy the ship! He knew it! At a single stroke he would get all the money he needed!

As he stumbled away, he looked gratefully towards Lord Marriner. His lordship was thoughtfully rubbing the silver knob of his stick against his cheek. He smiled at Peter, mildly. The lion and the lamb! The snarl and the smile. But how much bigger was the smile than the snarl! And – and next to the fierce little lion, the lamb was almost a monster!

'It must be perfect,' murmured his lordship. 'Your ship, I mean. No damage of any kind. We collectors are very particular, Mr Woodcock's boy. Why! we'd sooner destroy a damaged item than keep it in our house!'

'It's perfect – it's perfect!' Peter assured him eagerly. 'On my word of honour, your lordship!'

It was only when he'd left The Bedford Head, and was hurrying through the cold, dark streets, that a chill of doubt entered into him. What if the wretched little crime he'd just committed – the selling of the key – had already done some damage to his soul that would show up on the ship?

He broke into a run. He had to make sure. He didn't care if his soul had been holed below the water-line and was sinking fast, just so long as nothing showed up on his twenty-pound ship!

CHAPTER NINE

~~~~~~~~~~~~~

'What shall we do with the drunken sailor,
  What shall we do with the drunken sailor –'
Peter Gannet jumped a foot in the air, jerked his candle
and spilled hot wax over the shop counter and the bottle
containing his twenty-pound ship.
    'What shall we do with the drunken sailor,
      Earlie in the morning?'
It was Polly, singing like a bee. She must have come
down the stairs as quiet as a smell. She was standing right
behind him, holding her great shoes in one hand and a
mutton chop in the other. She sniffed at him.

'Pooh!' she said. 'You stink like a brewery! You ought
to be ashamed! Drinking at your age! What would your
ma say! Here!' she urged, poking the mutton chop under
his nose. 'Best get this down inside of you, else you'll be
having horrible dreams! Got to feed the inner boy. Got to
keep body and soul together, my lad!'

He put down his candle and took hold of the chop, but
more in self-defence than hunger.

'Eat up,' said Polly.

Reluctantly he took a bite and began to munch away,
but all the time looking anxiously at his ship. The bottle
was now speckled with wax, like white measles. He prayed
it hadn't done any damage.

So far as he could tell, from his brief examination before
Polly had come in, the ship was still all right. He'd been

worried about the topsails. Mr Velonty had said that one of the topsails on the other ship had come adrift, and it had struck him that it might have been due to a weakness that was common to both vessels; which, when he thought about it, was a good deal more likely than its being a sign that Paul's virtuous little soul was going to pot . . .

'Still dreaming of sailing away?' asked Polly, noticing the almost painful intensity of his stare at the ship. He finished chewing and took another bite. 'Now don't you go leaving the bone about,' warned Polly sternly. 'We don't want no rats and mice and suchlike vermin in the house.'

'That reminds me,' mumbled Peter, through meat; 'has Mr Velonty gone home yet?'

Polly wagged a reproachful finger.

'Don't you let the mistress hear you talking about her brother like that, my lad!' she said; then added, under her breath, *'But I can't say as the master would mind!'*

'Doesn't he like him, then?'

'I never said a word! You must be imagining things again! Too much to drink I 'spect. Anyway, he went off ages ago.'

Peter breathed a sigh of relief. He put down the chop and tried to scratch the spots of wax off the bottle with his fingernail.

'You're making it worse,' said Polly. 'Your fingers are all greasy. You go on eating and I'll clean it up for you.'

He watched her carefully as she picked up the ship, removed the spots with her thumbnail, and began to polish the glass with her apron.

'There!' she said, holding the ship up to her face and admiring the green shine she'd put on the glass. 'As good as new!'

He looked. He caught his breath. For a moment he'd fancied that there was a dark stain across the deck, like the beginning of a black rot. But then he saw it was only the shadow of one of Polly's fingers. Suddenly he could see St Elmo's Fire burning along the yards and up and down the spider-fine shrouds. He looked more closely. It was only the dancing reflection of his candle flame.

He studied the tiny hatches, the delicately scored planking of the decks; he searched among the pale tracery of masts for signs of imperfection . . . until he caught sight of Polly's large eyes, gleaming and glinting through the lines and stays in the soft yellow light, and drenching all the rigging with pearls.

'D'you know,' she murmured dreamily, 'if the sea was as flat as a table, and the water was as dry as a biscuit, I wouldn't mind sailing away meself, on a ship like this! Where shall we sail to? Margate . . . or Herne Bay?'

'To Zanzibar,' muttered Peter, feeling affronted by such domestic and commonplace dreams. 'To Zanzibar and the China Seas.'

Polly blinked mistily and the vessel heeled over and swung into the wind, as she turned the bottle to admire the little bone ship all round. She peered down on it; and if Sinbad the Sailor had been on the deck, and lashed to the mast as he usually was, and had looked up, and seen what was staring down, he'd have told a marvellous story about an enormous jug-faced genie that had risen up out of the sea and magically imprisoned him and his ship inside its own green glass bottle . . .

'That's queer!' said Polly suddenly.

'Why? What's wrong?'

'Nothing. Only didn't you tell me that your brother's got a ship just like this one?'

'Yes.'

'Then you've got the wrong one, my lad. He's got yours and you've got his. Careful!' she cried out, as he snatched the bottle out of her hands.

The old man had engraved the names of the ships under the stern galleries. The writing was tiny; Mr Bagley must have done it under a powerful magnifying-glass; but it was plain. The ship he'd got in his hands was the *Paul*! He'd got the wrong one!

He shook, he trembled! Tears of rage filled his eyes! He knew that Paul had done it on purpose. He'd changed the ships secretly. He remembered now the look on Paul's face as they'd said goodbye, the pathetic, sickly little smile that said, all too plainly, 'You'll never be free of me, Peter, never, never!' He'd sent the *Paul* to Cucumber Alley, while the *Peter* stayed behind in Hope Sufferance Wharf!

'Are you feeling sick?' asked Polly anxiously. 'You've gone as white as your candle! And you're shaking all over! It's the drink –'

Peter shook his head. He was all right – he was all right – Polly looked at him curiously. She shrugged her shoulders, picked up her shoes and the chop bone, and went back upstairs to finish clearing away the dinner table.

Peter pulled out his bed from under the counter and collapsed on it. His head was spinning and he felt sick with fright. He was thinking of the ship back at Hope Sufferance Wharf, the ship from which a topsail was already coming adrift. *His ship!* God knew what was happening to it now!

As the clocks of Covent Garden and the Strand were striking ten, and the iron gates of Cucumber Alley were locked, and Peter Gannet was beginning to think about what would happen if Dawkins was struck down dead in Newman Street and Stint's devil was empty in the morning, the bells of St Mary's in Rotherhithe likewise boomed and banged, and little Paul got up from his chair in the parlour of Gannet's chandlery, kissed his parents and Mrs Jiffy goodnight, and went upstairs to bed.

Mr and Mrs Gannet glanced at one another; and Mrs

Jiffy gave a sigh, small and neat as her stitching. Since Peter had gone away, life was quiet in the chandlery, and peaceful, too. Even so, you had to admit there was a gap in the chandlery days, a sense of loss ... although, all things considered, it was more like the gap felt by the loss of an aching tooth than anything else ...

'Poor soul!' murmured Mrs Jiffy, taking off her spectacles and laying aside a half-made hat; and for a moment, Mr Gannet wondered which of his sons she meant.

Paul's candle had been lit and there was a fire burning brightly in his grate. Briefly he warmed his hands, for he was a chilly mortal and felt the cold even on so short a journey as from the parlour to his room. He went to the chest of drawers, took down the ship and laid it carefully on the floor. Then he crouched down and stared at it, like an ever watchful crow.

The foretopsail, which, only a few hours before, had still been hanging to the yard, had now come away altogether. It had fallen and was caught in the shrouds like a dead sea-bird. As he was staring at it in bewilderment and distress, there came a knock on his door. It was Mrs Jiffy with his milk.

'The best thing, dear,' she said, when she saw what had happened, 'would be to ask Mr Bagley to put it back again. I'll mention it to your father –'

'– No, no!' cried Paul anxiously. 'Please don't do that! Mr Bagley's such an old man, isn't he! I – I don't want to trouble him! Please – Please don't say anything, Mrs Jiffy!'

'That's just like you, Paul, dear,' said Mrs Jiffy tenderly. 'Always thinking of others!'

When she'd gone, Paul sat down on his bed and clutched his head in his hands. It wasn't because he wanted to spare the old man labour that he didn't want Mrs Jiffy to say anything, it was because he was frightened. Although the name on the ship was much too small to be read by anybody at Hope Sufferance Wharf, the old man who'd made the ships would know it at once – like a father would know his own child – *and he'd know what had been done.*

Paul stood up and went to the fire again. He was freezing cold. He tried not to look up into the mirror above the mantelpiece; but he couldn't help himself.

'I hate you, Paul,' he whispered, as the waxen face of a poorly angel gazed meekly back at him. 'I hate you – I hate you!'

He went back to the chest of drawers, pulled out a drawer and took out the article that had brought about his last fight with Peter: the sailor's devil mask that had been given to him at Christmas.

He put it on and returned to the mirror. This time a gaudy demon with a beak for a nose peered back at him through the mysterious slits in its golden eyes. It was a wicked, horrible face, and, coming round a corner, would have made you jump. But somehow it made him feel strangely free. It was as if the sailor's devil mask was more comfortable to wear than the angel mask that Nature had printed on his face.

He felt much easier now about looking at the ship. Nevertheless, as he went back to it, his heart was fluttering like a bird's. Although he hadn't been able to hear much through the closed door of what had been said down in the shop when Mr Bagley had given the ships to Peter, he'd guessed, from the look on his brother's face, that there was something important about them. It had always been like that. Peter, strong, grinning, open-natured Peter, had never been able to hide anything from the secret eyes of Paul.

The beaky demon glared greedily at the little white ship, as if longing to gobble it up. Suddenly the demon jerked back and gave a muffled cry of dismay! There was more damage! Now the main topsail was hanging loose. It was as if a dark and terrible hurricane was blowing inside the green glass bottle, and blasting the little white ship to Kingdom Come!

The watcher, the crow in the crow's nest, rocked himself to and fro. But all he could do was to watch.

CHAPTER TEN

vwvwvwvwvw

Midnight had come and gone. Must have been more than half an hour ago. There was a wind in a devil of a hurry blowing down Cucumber Alley and making the great iron key that hung up outside the locksmith's creak and grunt as it swung back and forth on its chains. Eek . . . ugh! Eek . . . ugh! Eek . . .

Inside the shop, a pair of round, wide-open eyes, set unnaturally far apart on account of their being formed by the finger-holes in the shutters, stared down dully on the unsleeping apprentice . . . now silverishly watchful, now dim almost to the point of invisibility, as clouds kept drifting across the moon and changing the night. Eek . . . ugh! Eek . . . ugh! Eek –!

Peter Gannet sat up. He'd heard another sound, further off. It was a faint metallic click, with something furtive about it, such as might have been made by Dawkins cautiously turning another key in a well-oiled lock.

Following this, and for nearly a minute, there was nothing to be heard except for the wind and the grunting of the locksmith's sign. Eek . . . ugh! Eek . . . ugh! Eek –! Peter Gannet held his breath. Another sound, and much nearer at hand. It was a curious scraping and a soft wooden thump, such as might have been made by Dawkins putting the key inside Stint's devil and carefully shutting its head.

He lay back on his pillow, thinking desperately. If the sounds he'd heard had really been Dawkins coming back and putting the key inside Stint's devil, then it would be better to go and get it now, rather than risk waiting until morning. But the night was so wild that if he opened the door the horrible wind would be sure to rush in and wake up the whole house.

Suddenly, and it was as if he had fallen asleep and woken up again, he became aware that the wind had stopped. He thanked whoever had done it for him. He got out of bed, unbolted the door and opened it. The night was cold and pale and quiet. A few flakes of snow were drifting down. He crept outside, looked up and down the Alley, then crossed over on freezing tiptoe.

There was an iron ring set in the wall beside Stint's door, about two feet off the ground. It provided a conveni- ent foot-rest for reaching up to the little painted devil which, as its head was tipped back on its hinges, and Peter's hand fumbled inside, seemed to be roaring with silent laughter, as if the apprentice's searching fingers were tickling it.

'Bless you, Dawkins!' breathed Peter, climbing down again. The key had been inside the devil all right. Like Jay had said, Dawkins was a person of good faith.

He went back into the shop. Thoughtfully he propped the door open with a stool so he would have enough light to find his way from hiding-place to hiding-place.

The wind, coming down the chimney, had revived the dying furnace a little. The coals glowed fitfully and the workroom was all blood and shadows. He looked up at the wall of keys. It glimmered and glinted in an indistinct and dangerous confusion. One careless move would bring all the iron tumbling thunderously down! He shuddered at the thought. He needed more light. He fetched his candle and, with a pair of tongs, kindled it from a bright ember out of the fire.

As the flame tottered at the wick, he had a momentary

sensation of persons unseen suddenly darting back and hiding from him, in corners and under the bench. He licked his lips, which were unnaturally dry. Although he knew that it had only been the shadows shrinking back from the yellow light, he would, at that moment, gladly have given up all Dawkins's money for the night's business to have been finished with and himself back in bed. Next time, he vowed shakily, he'd ask for more ...

With enormous caution, and fearful that the very creaking of his bones would give him away, he climbed up on a stool and gently put back number seventeen on its empty nail. Thank God it was done! He climbed down again. He felt better, much better ... All that remained was to lock up the workroom and go back to bed.

He took a step towards the bench to pick up his candle. As he did so, he heard a faint noise. In an instant, he was an apprentice of stone! He stood, motionless, with his hand outstretched and one foot in the air, listening!

It was the strange clinking and jingling that he'd heard on his very first night in the locksmith's shop. It was in the air all round him, and, to his terrified ears, it sounded as loud as alarm bells!

It was the keys. Somehow or other he must have brushed against them and set them chiming against each other. He turned and peered anxiously up at the wall. But the keys hung still and silent, each in its little black pocket of shadow, while the jingling and clinking went on.

'Joey! Joey!'

A voice, thin as an eyelash, seemed to brush right against his cheek!

'W-*who's there?*' he breathed, not daring to look.

'Joey ... Joey!' he heard again; and then came a queer little cackling laugh that was close enough to touch!

'*Who's there – who's there?*' He turned –

'Tom!' It was behind him! Another voice whispering

down his neck! 'Tom Pulham, as I don't live and breathe!'

He turned again. There was no one there!

'Joey ... Joey Barnett! Where have you been all my death?'

'Under the hills and near at hand!' came the weird reply.

All at once, the workroom was full of whisperings, very dry and rustling, like a wind across dead leaves. The tinkling and jingling was louder now, and more distinct. It was no longer like keys, but more as if unseen glasses were being clinked together to celebrate invisible meetings with eerie toasts ...

'Drink up, drink up! Drink to me bony with thine eyes! Drink up, old friend ... Here's blood in your eye!'

Terrified, the apprentice turned and turned again, like a blind man frightened by moths, as the uncanny whisperings and soft laughter fluttered and fumbled all round him in the shadowy air. Suddenly his frantically searching gaze fell upon the wall of hands. He cried out in amazement! They were vanishing! Before his very eyes, the pallid hands were disappearing, one by one, off the wall!

'My hand, old friend, here's my hand! Here's to all of us, here's to all dead men and true!'

It was then that Peter Gannet knew what it was that was happening inside the locksmith's workroom, among the keys and files and hammers and rasps. It was the old custom; it was Hand next Heart. Just as Mr Shoveller had told him, the long-departed workmen had come back, for old time's sake, to drink a glass of ale, and claim their hands off the wall. But they were all dead, of course, dead and gone. The workroom was full of ghosts!

Peter Gannet, the chime-child, had come into his inheritance. The ghosts had come because of him. It was his mysterious power that had unlocked the grave and awakened the dead. His terror left him; and in its place he felt a great excitement and sense of boundless freedom. It was as if the walls of a prison in which he'd been shut up all his life had suddenly and quietly folded themselves away.

'Let me see you!' he whispered, stretching out his hands. 'The old man promised that I would *see* ghosts! I want to see you! I have a right –'

But even as he spoke, the whispering stopped. For some mysterious reason, the ghosts had fled, leaving behind in the workroom an iron silence, like the silence of double death.

Then, suddenly, and with a violent rush, the door burst open! Instantly an icy wind rushed in, tore at the candle flame and put it out. Then the silence returned.

There was someone standing in the doorway. In the dim red light afforded by the furnace coals, Peter saw that it was a figure all in black, hooded and without a face.

'W-who are you?' he whispered, almost dead with fright.

The figure made no answer. For a moment, it remained standing in the doorway; then, looking neither to the right nor the left – though in truth it seemed to have nothing, no glimmer of eyes inside its hood to look with – it moved across the workroom like black smoke, and stopped before the wall of hands. Who was it? What did it want, this late-coming ghost of the workroom night? The wall was bare; all the hands had gone. EXCEPT FOR ONE! Just under the window there still remained the dead-white fingers of Thomas Kite, the hated *other one*!

'So it's you!' breathed Peter, as the hooded figure raised its arm to claim the last hand. 'So you're dead, too!'

Then a horrible thing happened! The phantom's sleeve had fallen back; and it was empty! It had no arm, it had no hand! It could not claim the hand off the wall!

It tried again, and again, uselessly. It kept flapping and beating against the wall, like a bird with a broken wing; and each time its sleeve fell back, empty. At last it abandoned its efforts. It drew away from the wall and every fold of its darkness expressed despair. It drifted back across the workroom, hovered briefly before the wall of keys, and passed through the open door. As it went, the dead apprentice gestured to the living one. Once, twice, three times it beckoned with its empty sleeve. Follow me ... follow ... follow ...

It passed through the shop, that it must have known so well, and out into Cucumber Alley beyond. Follow, follow, follow, beckoned the empty sleeve. It was bitterly cold outside and the snow was falling faster. You could see the flakes fluttering and swirling inside the phantom, like white butterflies in a black net.

For a moment, it remained motionless outside Stint's; then, as if alarmed by something, it hastened along the Alley towards the gates. When it reached them, it paused again; but only for long enough to jerk and beckon with increased urgency; follow, follow, follow ... Then it passed through the close-wrought iron like thin black soup.

Peter Gannet could go no further. Dawkins, that person of principle and good faith, had been careful to lock the gates. All that the half-frozen Peter Gannet could do was to stare and stare through the iron-work as the beckoning phantom dwindled away into nothingness, leaving behind it a curious, but not unpleasant, smell of seaweed and fish ... as if Thomas Kite had died of drowning, with all his crimes for company. They must have been dark indeed, thought Peter sombrely, as he returned to the locksmith's shop. Even the dead had shunned him; and he'd lost the right to claim his hand.

CHAPTER ELEVEN

vwvwvwvwvw

A ghost that stank of fish? What a preposterous notion, as Mr Velonty would say!

The haunted apprentice, lying in his narrow bed behind the counter, and watching the early morning begin to creep into the shop through the cracks and holes in the shutters, struggled with his recollections of the night.

What kind of fish, Gannet, eh, eh? Cod? Mackerel? Haddock . . . or good red herring? Answer me, boy, answer me!

Cautiously he sniffed the stale air; then he sat up and stared long and hard at the quiet workroom door, while the schoolmaster inside his aching head continued to pour scorn on his mysteries.

Fried, boiled or pickled, Gannet?

He grinned feebly, as he always did when Mr Velonty was sarcastic; and stayed in bed waiting for sounds of Polly stirring upstairs. Dully he remembered her warning about the consequences of boozing in The Bedford Head. Bad dreams. But everything had seemed so real. He could remember every detail; and the weird smell of the phantom still lingered in his nostrils. All the same, he had to admit that it was more likely that the workroom ghosts and the fishy phantom had come out of a bottle than out of the grave.

Something of the kind had happened to him once before, he remembered, when Mr Purvis had come to dinner at the chandlery and, before Mrs Gannet could stop him, had tipped a spoonful of brandy over Peter's pudding, 'just to liven it up, ma'am'. He'd had a bad night after that. He'd dreamed that he'd killed his brother Paul with a stone, like Cain and Abel, and had been digging a hole in St Mary's churchyard to hide the corpse, when he'd woken up, sweating with terror. That dream, he remembered, had been so strong and real in every particular that, when he'd seen that Paul was still in bed and alive, he'd almost wept with relief!

Suddenly a disturbing thought struck him. If the beckoning phantom and the whispering ghosts had only been a dream, then maybe his visit to the workroom itself had been a dream? Maybe his freezing scamper through the snow and stealthy returning of the key to its nail had only happened inside his sleeping head? If so, then number seventeen was still outside in Stint's devil!

His heart began to thump with anxiety. He got out of bed and dressed himself at high speed. He paused for a moment and listened. The house was still quiet. Cautiously he unbolted the shop door and opened it. He stared. The world was white. If he'd dreamed the snow, then so had the weather, to a depth of about two inches. Cucumber Alley was no more than a pen-and-ink sketch on white paper: indistinct outlines of shops and a vague grey scribble to mark the scurrying of a cat. Stint's devil was wearing a white hat and had a white parcel in its lap, like a Christmas present . . .

The locksmith's apprentice glanced furtively up and down the Alley, then darted across to Stint's, climbed up on the iron ring, and opened up the devil. It was empty. He climbed down again, uneasily. Either Dawkins had dropped down dead in Newman Street with the key still in his pocket, or –

The window above the devil shot open and dislodged a

quantity of snow. Peter looked up, and Ruby Stint looked down. Gone were her smiles; her brown hair was falling all round her accusing face like a fringe round a crumpled cushion.

'I saw you,' she said.

'W-what do you mean?'

For answer, a portly hand came out, pointed down to the devil, and then made an unmistakable gesture of a key turning in a lock.

'You'll be for it,' she said. 'You and all the others. Dawkins and Jay and – and Robbins and the rest of them.'

'I – I don't know what you're talking about.'

'I wish you'd never come,' said Ruby Stint, her black-currant eyes all squashy with resentment and grief. 'It was all right before you came.'

'Why? I've never done you any harm!'

Ruby Stint sniffed. 'When they couldn't get out at night,' she said, 'they used to come courting me. Now you've spoilt it all.'

Before he could say anything, she'd vanished from view and shut the window with a bang. It was plain that she didn't care if she woke up all Cucumber Alley. Now she was back on the shelf again, Cucumber Alley could go hang itself; and so could all the apprentices in it.

Peter Gannet stood outside the jeweller's, breathing deeply. Steam came out of him in puffs, like an apprentice on the boil. He felt indignant. Ruby Stint's blaming him for her misfortunes was grossly unfair. He scowled heavily; then, experiencing a twinge of philosophy, he shrugged his shoulders and reflected that you needed to be dead before you could go about your business without inconveniencing somebody or other. He sighed and trudged back across the Alley, carefully kicking up the snow in order to destroy the tell-tale footprints that led, loud and black, from the locksmith's shop straight to the devil.

77

Briefly he glanced back towards the window from which the fat girl of sorrows had looked down. He remembered her sombre words. 'You'll be for it,' she'd said. Uncomfortably he wondered if her threat had meant that she'd been to the devil before him and had taken away the key out of female spite; for was it not common knowledge that hell has no fury like a woman scorned?

The more he thought about it, the more likely it seemed, and he fell into a violent rage against the jeweller's daughter that lasted until Mr Shoveller arrived and opened up the workroom. Then, to his enormous relief, Peter saw that number seventeen was back on its nail and the white hands were back on the wall. So one part of what had happened in the night – his returning of the key – must have been real; but what of the rest of it?

At eleven o'clock, Peter escaped from the horrible, stifling workroom, with its never-ending banging and rasping and screaming of iron, and the never-ending mumblings and mutterings and complainings of Mr Shoveller. It was time to fetch the old fool's ale.

Outside, in Cucumber Alley, the neat snow was a crumpled ruin, like a sheet after a nightmare; and muffled passers-by crept hither and thither, like cautious beetles in boots. Ruby Stint was at her window again; and Peter, inwardly begging her pardon for having previously maligned her in his thoughts, saluted her courteously before hastening on to the public-house at the corner of Neal's Yard.

There was good news waiting for him. More money. Dawkins, like some flour-faced Sinbad, had told such a tale of his marvellous adventures in the soft arms of Miss Harrison that the very froth on the waiting ale had gasped and blinked; and Robbins, from Armitage and Ware, the bootmaker's on The Sin, had been so inflamed that he was ready to part with his life's savings for a visit to Newman Street like Dawkins's. He wanted the key.

'Tonight,' said Jay, the great arranger, who regarded himself as the father of the Alley and was generally looked up to, even though he was as short as a fart. 'Half-past eight in The Bedford Head. All right with you, young Gannet?'

Peter nodded.

'That's the ticket!' said Jay approvingly. 'None of that twisting and turning, like that bleeding corkscrew Thomas Kite, eh?'

'You can say that again!' muttered Peter Gannet with an involuntary shudder; and took a quick swig of Mr Shoveller's ale.

On the way back, he thought about The Bedford Head and the possibility of seeing Lord Marriner again, which was the only reason he'd agreed so readily to Jay's arrangements. It certainly wasn't on account of Robbins's paltry sixpence that he was willing to go through all the frantic terrors of getting the key again. He wondered if he ought to take the ship with him when he went to The Bedford Head. After all, as Mr Shoveller was always saying, it's best to strike while the iron's hot. On the other hand, his lordship might regard it as an impertinence for a locksmith's boy to try and sell him a ship in a bottle in a public place, and take offence; so perhaps it would be better to wait for Lord Marriner to make the first move. He'd mentioned doing favours, Peter remembered, so he must have had something in mind . . .

As he drew level with Stint's, he looked up at the window again. The jeweller's daughter had gone, and the jeweller's devil grinned. He peered in at the shop window, which, as usual, was blazing like a bonfire with gold and jewels; and couldn't help thinking that a brick through the glass, a quick fistful, then a brisk trot to Tilbury, and all his troubles would be over.

Somebody was standing next to him. He'd just noticed, out of the corner of his eye, that he was no longer alone. He didn't turn to take a closer look as he supposed it was only some passer-by who, like a moth, had been attracted to Stint's showy window. Instead, he continued to stand, musing idly about Tilbury and bricks. Then, little by little, he got the impression that the newcomer was taking an interest in a particular item that was lying right in the front of the window, a gold bracelet fairly peppered with pearls and emeralds that must have been worth a fortune. Gannet grinned inwardly as he wondered if his half-seen companion's thoughts were the same as his own. He waited, hopefully; but as nothing happened, he turned to go back to his place of employment with Mr Shoveller's long-overdue ale.

As he did so, the figure moved. Peter Gannet caught an indistinct glimpse of an arm being raised. For a moment, he wondered breathlessly if a brick was really about to be thrown. But the arm had been raised for a different purpose. Once, twice, three times it beckoned; and the air was full of the smell of seaweed and fish!

It was the phantom, the stinking phantom from the workroom! It had come out of the night to haunt him, even in the broad and pitiless light of day! His ghosts had been real. His mysterious powers had indeed drawn Thomas Kite from the grave. And he wouldn't go back!

The locksmith's apprentice stood stock-still. He glared blindly across the Alley while Mr Shoveller's ale slopped and danced in the pot as the hand that clutched it shook and trembled like mad. He couldn't move. They say the lady in the Bible was turned into a pillar of salt by looking back at the horror behind her. Peter Gannet hadn't needed to look back; he'd been turned into something equally white and motionless by the thought alone!

Suddenly the locksmith's door opened and Mr Woodcock came out. Peter Gannet's terror took another turn, and very much for the worse. He was instantly convinced that if his master so much as glimpsed the dead apprentice he would immediately know everything about the living one!

Frantically he tried to hold out his arms, to lean sideways, in short, to do anything to obstruct the locksmith's view. But, thank God! Mr Woodcock had other matters on his mind. Without so much as a glance in the direction of Stint's, he turned to go into the Propagation next door. In another moment, he would have been inside among the Bibles and safely out of the way; but even as he stretched out his hand to the door, a customer came out and nearly fell over him.

'I'm sorry, ma'am, . . . oh, I'm sorry . . . so – so sorry, ma'am!' he heard Mr Woodcock stammer, in a foolish, flustered kind of way, more like a boy caught cheating than his iron grim employer; while the customer, a stately, stuck-up cow in black furs, shrugged off the hand put out to help her.

'Oh for God's sake, get on with it!' screamed Peter, inside his head, for the turning and dancing about in the doorway seemed to be going on forever. Then at last Mr Woodcock, with poppies in his cheeks, shambled into the Propagation and the customer stalked away.

She was coming across the Alley, straight for Gannet. She stopped. For an instant, he thought she'd seen the ghost. Her face was white and her eyes were enormous. But it was Gannet she was looking at.

'What are you staring at me like that for, boy?' she demanded, her voice absolutely shaking with anger. 'Are you mad, or what?' She gestured to dismiss him; and, as she did so, she dropped the book she had bought in the Propagation.

'I – I –' began Peter, when he felt himself poked in the back and then thrust irritably to one side. It was Mr Stint who'd come out of his shop like it was on fire.

The fat little jeweller, muttering something about 'mannerless lout', hastened to pick up the book, wipe the snow off it, and return it to the lady with a respectful duck of his head.

'Boys these days, m'lady!' he murmured. 'Little ruffians! No respect! No proper eddication!'

'Thank you, Mr Stint,' said the lady. 'I'm obliged to you.' She glanced at Gannet. 'I thought he was ill or something. He was standing so – so peculiarly.'

'Mr Woodcock's new boy,' explained Mr Stint, as if anxious to shift the blame; and then, to Peter: 'Be off with you, Gannet!'

Peter nodded, but didn't move. He was almost sure the phantom had gone. The weird smell of seaweed and fish had faded away and in its place was a perfume of roses that came off the lady in waves. The old cow must have poured it on by the pint . . .

'I said, be off with you, Gannet!' repeated Mr Stint. 'Don't just stand there like a block of wood! I've half a mind to tell your master about your ruffianly behaviour to Lady Marriner!'

Gannet gave a stupid grin and, finding that his power of motion was restored, tottered feebly back to the locksmith's shop. His legs felt as weak as a baby's. So the old cow had been Lady Marriner, the pride of his lordship's collection! He wished he was dead.

He clumped into the workroom and gave Mr Shoveller his ale. The old misery peered into the pot, and, as usual, complained about how much had been spilled.

'The other one,' he grunted, 'wouldn't have lost a drop.

He had a hand on him what was steady as a rock.'

'Well, he ain't got one now, you old fool!' muttered Peter under his breath. 'All that's left of him is a stink and an empty sleeve!'

CHAPTER TWELVE

vwvwvwvwvw

'Lost a sixpence and found a penny, young Gannet?' inquired Mr Shoveller, observing, as he could hardly fail to do, the apprentice's dull and sunken looks, and the listless way he went about his daily tasks of sweeping, polishing, keeping the furnace going and waiting on the journeyman, hand and foot.

It was nearly half-past one; and the two hours that had passed in the workroom had been as grim and iron-footed a pair as ever tramped around a clock.

'Missing your folks, are you?'

Peter shook his head and rubbed at a brass plate as if it was a memory he wanted to wipe out. Far from missing Hope Sufferance Wharf, the very thought of it only added to his leaden despair. His world had collapsed. His inheritance, his strange, chime-child's inheritance, which had been the only thing he'd possessed of any distinction, had, like most inheritances, fallen somewhat short of expectation. His promised ghosts had turned out to be nothing more wonderful than the dreary shades of humble workmen and a dishonest apprentice; and, no doubt, his devil – if and when it should put in an appearance – would turn out to be just as mean, shabby and humdrum. But then, as Mr Velonty would have said, what more could be expected of a boy like Peter Gannet, a boy with no deep feelings and as thick as a post? He sighed.

'A girl, is it?' pursued Mr Shoveller, squinting at him

through a shiny keyhole. 'Some bit of fluff back in Rotherhithe you was sweet on?'

Again he shook his head, and threw a shovelful of iron sweepings onto the fire, where, like his dreams, they blazed up and went out almost at once. His thoughts turned to Lord Marriner and the bright hope he'd had of getting twenty pounds. Well, that hope, like the burning specks of iron, had gone out like all the rest. He'd behaved, as that interfering swine Mr Stint had pointed out, like a ruffian to his lordship's wife. Painfully and all too clearly, he remembered the look of pale outrage on Lady Marriner's face; and he could almost hear her telling her husband about the ill-mannered lout she'd met in Cucumber Alley that morning, who, thanks to Mr Stint, she'd found out was Mr Woodcock's new boy, name of Gannet ... His lordship would not have been pleased. Peter shrank inwardly, and in his mind's eye he could see Lord Marriner's gentle smile turn into the silver snarl of the little lion on the top of his walking-stick, as he heard about the unlucky insult to his wife. Peter groaned ...

'Got the belly-ache, then?' suggested Mr Shoveller, filing away at the keyhole and blowing through it with a whistling noise. 'A good dose of rhubarb, lad. That'll clear you out.'

Rhubarb. Perhaps Mr Shoveller was right, and all that was needed for a boy like him was a good dose of rhubarb to clear out all the dark and disagreeable things inside him.

'Shift a house,' Mr Shoveller assured him; but before he could go on, a customer came into the shop.

Mr Shoveller cocked his head and listened, to make sure that the master had heard the doorbell. He had. Mr Woodcock's heavy feet came thumping down the stairs and there followed a murmuring of voices, after which the customer departed and the shop door banged shut. A moment later, Mr Woodcock came into the workroom. He was holding up part of a broken key.

'It's number a hundred and eighteen, Mr Shoveller,' he said. 'Wanted this afternoon. Can you manage?'

Mr Shoveller took the broken key, squinted at it, then shuffled over to the wall and lifted down number a hundred and eighteen.

'Cabinet key, ain't it, master?'

'That's right, Mr Shoveller.'

'Pity he didn't bring the other half,' grunted Mr Shoveller, frowning at the broken piece which consisted only of the stem and bow. 'If he'd brought the terminals we could have let him have our one, and I could have made up the other in our own time.'

'Folk don't always think of us, Mr Shoveller.'

Mr Shoveller shrugged his shoulders. 'What time's he coming back for it?'

'He wants it delivered, Mr Shoveller.'

'Where to, master? Seeing as how it's Saturday, I s'pose it's the other end of the world!'

'It's only in Bow Street, Mr Shoveller. Lord Marriner's –'

The apprentice started, and accidentally knocked a rasp off the bench. Mr Shoveller scowled and muttered something about a clumsy ox, then said he'd deliver the key himself on his way home.

'No need for that, Mr Shoveller. The boy can go. In fact, that was the message his lordship sent. According to the fellow who brought the key, his lordship was very particular about not wanting to inconvenience you or me. Tell them to send the boy with it, he said. So you see, Mr Shoveller, they do think of us sometimes.'

The key was ready at half-past four and Peter Gannet, well wrapped up against the biting cold, set off for Bow

86

Street. Of all places in the world, he could think of none that appealed to him less, at that moment, than number twenty-seven, Bow Street. He felt in his bones that Lord Marriner had only asked for the boy to be sent, not because he didn't want to inconvenience Mr Woodcock or Mr Shoveller, but because he *did* want to inconvenience Peter Gannet. He could see it all. Lord Marriner would be waiting for him, sitting in an enormous chair, and Lady Marriner would be standing beside him, glaring. 'Is this the boy?' his lordship would demand, pointing his stick straight at Gannet. 'Yes,' her ladyship would reply, smiling cruelly. 'That's the little ruffian!'

The day was beginning to fade; and the lamps in the shop windows, shining out over the pocked and pitted snow, turned it as sick and yellow as an old man's crumpled skin. Peter Gannet caught sight of Robbins, the bootmaker's apprentice, industriously shovelling away the dirty snow that had piled up outside Armitage and Ware's.

Robbins's eyes were bright as buttons, and his round face was flushed with eagerness and excitement. Gannet knew why. Robbins was thinking about his forthcoming night in Newman Street with Miss Harrison. The thought crossed Peter's mind of letting him off the sixpence in exchange for a favour. If Robbins was to take the cabinet key to Bow Street in place of Gannet, then, when Lord Marriner asked, 'Is this the boy?' Lady Marriner would have to say, 'No. That is not the boy!' and the identity of the ill-mannered lout of Cucumber Alley would remain shrouded in mystery.

But it was too late. Even as Peter was still considering the possibility, Robbins, having finished with the snow, performed a furtively suggestive little dance with his shovel, kissed it, and went back inside the shop. Peter turned his back and tramped away.

He shivered; not because of the biting cold, which meant little to a boy like him, but because he was really frightened. It wasn't that Peter Gannet was a coward. Far from it. In the dangerous world of streets and boys, he was somebody to be reckoned with, inasmuch as he never avoided a fight and frequently started one. But people in authority were different. Somehow they always made him feel helpless and guilty, even when there wasn't any need; and in the person of a lord, authority loomed even larger and more menacing than it did in the persons of his schoolmaster or his employer. Consequently, as he trudged along Bow Street and stopped outside number twenty-seven, he was frightened half out of his wits.

He crept up the front steps, knocked faintly on the door, and, as soon as it was opened, attempted to push the key into the footman's hand, with a view – having made his delivery – to departing as fast as was humanly possible.

But the swine of a footman was having none of it. He waved the key aside and said that his lordship wanted to make sure it fitted properly. He said his lordship was waiting for Mr Woodcock's boy, so would Mr Woodcock's boy be good enough to step this way ... 'And take off your cap, lad!'

His lordship was somewhere in among his collection. He must have been, because the footman said, 'Mr Woodcock's boy, m'lord,' and left the room and shut the door behind him. But after that, nothing, except for the ticking of an unseen clock.

Mr Woodcock's boy waited. He didn't dare to move. Lord Marriner's multitudinous collection loomed and lurked and crowded dangerously all round him. Spindly tables nudged him; huge heavy pictures seemed about to topple down on him; bronze animals, prowling through silver forests of candlesticks, snarled at him; and marble women glared.

Cautiously, Mr Woodcock's boy tried to shift his big dirty boots off the flower-garden that was embroidered all over the carpet. Instantly, a crowd of china figures in a cabinet pressed forward to see what he was up to; and in the gleaming, tall glass doors, the nervously peering locksmith's boy himself was weirdly reflected, as if he, too, had been collected . . .

'So we meet again, young man!'

With a shock, Peter realized that Lord Marriner had been sitting all the time in a tremendous leather chair by the fire; and, like everything else in the room, was watching him. But, thank God! there was no Lady Marriner . . . although, in a room like his lordship's, you couldn't be sure.

'You've brought me the key?'

He was smiling. He was actually smiling! Although it was hard to believe, Lord Marriner seemed pleased to see him! Was it possible after all that the old cow hadn't told him anything about the ill-mannered lout in Cucumber Alley? Peter Gannet felt his usual stupid grin begin to spread helplessly over his face, so that, for a moment, the lord and the apprentice were smiling at one another, almost like old friends.

His lordship beckoned and Peter, trying not to tread too heavily on the carpet, approached and held out the key. Somewhat fastidiously, Lord Marriner extracted the key from the boy's shaking hand and began to examine it, while Peter tried to hide the dark blots his boots had left on the flower-garden. His lordship looked up. He cocked his head to one side.

'The door!' he said sharply. 'Go and make sure it's properly shut. I felt a draught.'

Peter went to the door, feeling that Lord Marriner was

watching him all the way ... most likely because he wanted to make sure that nothing valuable disappeared into the apprentice's pocket.

His lordship must have been imagining things. The door was properly shut. Nevertheless, Peter tried the handle. As he did so, he thought he heard a faint rustling on the other side, as if somebody had moved away, quickly.

'That's better!' said his lordship when the boy returned. 'Cold air, you know, can be as dangerous to a valuable collection as –' he laughed – 'as it is to a lady's delicate face!'

He stood up and, leaning slightly on his stick, went over to the cabinet. Anxiously, Mr Woodcock's boy waited to be dismissed. But his lordship was in no hurry.

'Strange,' he murmured, staring down at the key in his hand as if he'd just been struck by something peculiar about it, 'how the other one broke! I just dropped it in the fireplace and it snapped in two! Would you believe it!' He looked Peter straight in the eye, almost as if he was challenging the boy to call him a liar. 'Look!' he said, fumbling awkwardly in his waistcoat pocket. 'Here's the other half! Snapped off clean!'

Peter, uncomfortably feeling that he ought to defend his trade, repeated what Mr Shoveller had said about its being a pity his lordship hadn't sent the terminals as then he could have had the key off the wall right away, and not had to wait so long –

'– Of course, of course!' exclaimed his lordship, striking his forehead with the palm of his hand. 'I forgot that Mr Woodcock keeps a copy of all the keys he's made! Hm! a tremendous collection, eh? And so wise! If you know the number, it must be so easy to find the right key! But never mind, never mind! Everything's turned out for the best! Here we are together, young man, and we can talk about your fine ship in the bottle, eh?'

The clock ticked, the fire chuckled, and Peter Gannet, speechless as a block of wood, grinned like an idiot. He couldn't believe it! Only five minutes before – not even five minutes! – he'd been sunk in utter darkness and despair; and now, in the twinkling of an eye, the sun was shining, birds were singing, and he was as good as on his way to Zanzibar and the China Seas! Such was the power of a man like Lord Marriner!

'You still want to sell it, young man?' inquired his lordship anxiously. 'You haven't forgotten our little talk in The Bedford Head?'

Peter Gannet shook his head violently; and silently cursed himself for not having brought the ship with him. Lord Marriner looked pleased, and confessed that he'd taken quite a fancy to the idea of a ship in a bottle. He unlocked the cabinet, and the reflected apprentice trembled and fled off the edge of the glass as he opened the door.

'Tell me, young man,' he murmured, beginning to rearrange some figures on one of the shelves, 'do you think your ship would look well in here?'

Wonderingly, Peter nodded. Nobody had ever asked him for his opinion before; and for the first time in his life, that lout, that blockhead, that idle ruffian Peter Gannet, felt that somebody understood his true worth . . .

'Ah! I see you have a good eye, young man!'

His lordship had noticed that Peter was staring at a miniature that was lying on the shelf below. Carefully he lifted it out, with the odd effect of making a pair of china hares, that stood on either side of it, seem to jerk bolt-upright in alarm.

'There!' he said, displaying the tiny picture in the palm of his hand. 'You showed excellent taste to admire it. Of all my treasures, this is the one I value most. It is the real pride of my collection. It is Lady Marriner, of course . . .'

The picture represented a prettyish young woman with

black hair and pearls. With the best will in the world, Peter Gannet found it hard to see much of a likeness between her and the stuck-up cow who'd glared at him in Cucumber Alley. The passing of years hadn't exactly improved Lady Marriner; but then, Peter thought charitably, his lordship was very fond of antiques, so he must have thought about her differently.

But it wasn't the picture itself that had interested him, it was the frame. It was speckled all round with tiny pearls and emeralds, just like the bracelet he'd seen in Stint's window. It was a real coincidence, and, after properly praising the picture, he mentioned it.

'Indeed?' remarked his lordship, replacing the miniature and busying himself again with the figures on the shelf above. 'In Mr Stint's window?'

'Yes, your lordship. I saw it there only this morning.'

'In Mr Stint's window, you say?' he repeated, absently stroking a little country girl in a blue dress with a basket of yellow eggs balanced on her head. 'I must tell Lady Marriner about it. I'm sure she would like to see it.'

'Oh but she has! I mean, she must have seen it!'

'Why do you say that?'

'She – I mean, her ladyship came out of the Bible shop just as I was looking at it and nearly knocked into Mr Woodcock and –'

He stopped. There had been a sudden thump. It was the country girl. Lord Marriner's hand must have jerked, and the poor girl, taken by surprise, had toppled over sideways. His lordship frowned and set the figure upright again; and there was a frightened rush of reflections in the glass as he closed the cabinet door.

'In Cucumber Alley? This morning?'

'Yes, your lordship, she was –'

'No, no! Not her ladyship!' interposed Lord Marriner quickly. 'I meant the bracelet! I was thinking about the bracelet. I wasn't asking about Lady Marriner. We mustn't pry into ladies' little secrets, young man! But what am I saying! I don't need to tell a locksmith's boy about secrets! They're the very life's blood of his trade! All those keys! Amazing! Why, if you'd a mind to, I dare say you could find any key for any lock! Isn't that so?'

'I – I –'

'– But what am I thinking of, young man! Here you are, wanting only to talk about your ship and twenty pounds, while I chatter on about something else altogether! But you've put such an idea into my head – with your talk about keys and – and Mr Stint's bracelet! Shall I tell you what it is?'

Peter nodded, feeling that somehow his twenty pounds was in the balance. But his lordship didn't say anything. He was staring intently into the cabinet and his smooth, fleshy face, reflected in the glass door, mingled with the crowding china figures, so that it seemed full of delicate arms and legs and little china smiles, like some weird monster. He shook his head. It was the draught again. He'd felt it quite distinctly. He'd be obliged if Peter would try the door again. Sometimes it came open of its own accord . . .

It was firmly shut. As before, Peter tried the handle to make sure; and as before, he thought he heard a faint rustling on the other side. He wondered if he ought to say anything about it, but when he got back, his lordship immediately started talking about his idea.

Mr Stint's bracelet. He was going to buy it for Lady Marriner. But secretly. That was his idea. It was to be a great surprise. She was to know nothing about it, absolutely nothing! He spoke so quick and soft, and brought his large face so near to Peter's, that his warm, peppermint breath seemed to fold up the locksmith's boy in an invisible web.

He trusted Peter to keep his secret. That was important. After all, he didn't want to be disappointed in a boy who expected twenty pounds off him. He trusted Peter not to say anything . . . not even to his friends or to Mr Woodcock. These things get out, you know! It was to be a secret just between the two of them, between Master Gannet and Lord Marriner! There, now! That was something, eh? He smiled; and his eyes winked and twinkled like money in creased-up purses.

It was to be a seven-day secret. Only seven days. It was all to come out next Saturday. That was Lord and Lady Marriner's wedding anniversary. He wanted Lady Marriner to open her jewel-box first thing on the Saturday morning and, lo and behold! what do you suppose she would see?

'Mr Stint's bracelet!' whispered Peter Gannet, trying not to breathe in his lordship's face.

His lordship nodded appreciatively. Master Gannet was a quick-witted boy, he said; and Peter's thoughts flew to that pig Mr Velonty, and how he would have stared! Then his lordship said that everything depended on the locksmith's boy. Without the help of the locksmith's boy, nothing could be accomplished.

There was only one key in the house to Lady Marriner's jewel-box, and she always kept it with her. But, if what Master Gannet had told him was true, there must be another one hanging up in Mr Woodcock's shop. All that was needed, as Master Gannet himself had confirmed, was to know the right number –

'A hundred and twenty!' breathed his lordship. 'I want you to bring it to me on Friday. Lady Marriner will be out all that day. The last Friday in the month . . . always her day for visiting the – the sick, she tells me. She comes back quite worn-out from her labours, poor woman! But she sleeps very soundly, so we won't disturb her. But come late, Master Gannet. After midnight. We don't want the servants to be awake. We must keep our little secret, eh? Or – or am I asking too much of you?'

He paused and looked anxiously at the locksmith's boy. Was he asking too much? The clock ticked and the fire whispered; but the locksmith's boy just grinned, while his blunt, sturdy fingers busied themselves with wringing his cap, like a chicken's neck.

What a question! Asking too much indeed! Master Gannet was no ordinary, thick-witted street boy! Master Gannet was a boy with all his wits about him, a boy who would go far in the world. (To Zanzibar and the China Seas, please God! thought Peter, longingly.)

So it was settled. it was to be after midnight on Friday. His lordship would be waiting. But there was to be no noisy knocking on the door. It would wake the whole household. Safest to use the house key. It was number a hundred. Easy to remember, and – (his lordship chuckled mischievously) – and surely as easy to get two keys as one!

'And most important of all,' said his lordship, his gaze straying back to the cabinet, 'bring your fine ship with you. That way we can kill two birds with one stone, Master Gannet, eh? Strange, don't you think, how often it turns out that one kindness is rewarded by another! Yes, I'm really looking forward to buying your ship from you! It is perfect, you said? You are sure it is perfect?'

'Oh yes, yes, your lordship! Masts, sails, yards, rigging . . . everything!'

'It must be perfect! I will not have anything in my collection that is not perfect! A single fault, just one! would be like a cancer! It would poison everything! Why, I'd sooner –'

He stopped, and frowned. He opened the cabinet again and took out the pretty little country girl with the basket of eggs on her head. He examined her closely. He shook his head and gave her to Peter.

'Here! Your eyes are younger than mine. The basket on her head. Was it damaged when she fell? I think it was.'

He was right. There was a tiny chip off the edge of the basket; but it was no bigger than a pin's head.

'It's very small, your lordship. It hardly shows –'

'– Give her to me.'

He took the china girl and held her in the palm of his hand. Then he lifted his lion-headed stick and, with a sudden violent blow, smashed her into pieces!

'I cannot abide damaged goods!' he muttered.

He crossed the room and threw the fragments of coloured china into the fire. He stood for a moment, leaning on his stick and staring down into the flames. Then he turned back to the startled locksmith's boy and recollected that it was high time that the boy was getting back to his master's shop. Mr Woodcock would be wondering what had happened to him, he said.

Just before Peter left, Lord Marriner gave him a pound. He said it was on account of the twenty Peter would be getting on Friday. It was a gesture of good faith.

CHAPTER THIRTEEN

vvvvvvvvvvvv

Peter Gannet, head down and boots goings like hammers, hastened back to Cucumber Alley. He was sick with worry. The smashing of the china girl had upset him badly. He could still see the pitiful handful of broken pieces, and he was filled with alarm for the safety of his ship. Please God, let nothing have happened to it! he prayed, dreading that the smallest defect would bring the terrible lion-headed stick crashing down to reduce the little bone ship to a splintered ruin.

It was a horrible thought; not because of the possible loss of the twenty pounds, nor even because the ship was really Paul's and, if old Mr Bagley was right, its destruction might bring about the sinking of his brother's soul. That was the least of his worries. It was because of the ship itself. He couldn't bear to think of Mr Bagley's wonderful workmanship being smashed into pieces and thrown on the fire.

Mr Shoveller had gone and Mr Woodcock was locking up the workroom.

'I hear you're down in the dumps, lad,' said the master locksmith, squinting at the returned apprentice like he was a lock that needed oiling. 'But not to worry. It's only natural. When I was an apprentice,' he went on, his long face grinding itself up into a locksmith's smile, 'I cried my eyes out for the whole of my first month. But it passed. Everything passes, lad. It's part of growing up. Just give it time. This time next week, I shouldn't wonder, you'll be laughing . . .'

This time next week! As soon as the old fool had finished drivelling on about when he was a boy and had at last lumbered off upstairs, Gannet rushed to his cupboard and took out the ship. Anxiously he peered inside the green glass world where the white ship sailed. One by one, he examined the tiny poop lanterns and the delicate companionways. Then he searched among the pale masts and yards, and the soaring shrouds up which the sailors would have swarmed . . .

He nearly dropped the bottle! He'd caught a whiff of fish. Instantly a rush of fury overwhelmed him, a wild fury against the dead apprentice who wouldn't leave him alone!

'Keep away from me, Thomas Kite!' he screamed inside his head. 'Keep your stinking empty sleeve to yourself!'

But it wasn't the phantom after all. It was only Polly with a bit of haddock she'd saved up for him from tea.

'Here!' she said, shoving the plate under his nose. 'We've got to feed the inner boy.' She took the bottle out of his hands and put it on the counter so that he could hold the plate. 'Eat up,' she said. 'We've got to keep body and soul together, my lad!'

While the ship in Cucumber Alley sailed on untroubled through its green dreams, the ship in the upstairs room of the chandlery at Hope Sufferance Wharf heaved and staggered in nightmares! The damage was frightful. Not only had the main topsail quite fallen away, but, half-way up the mainmast itself, thin and black as a spider's leg, was a crack! Ruin was spreading through the vessel like a disease!

Quietly, the beaked demon, that had been glaring at it

through mysterious golden slits, put the little ship away in the chest of drawers.

'Paul, dear!' came Mrs Jiffy's voice from the landing below. 'Dinner is nearly ready, my angel!'

The demon took off its face; and Paul Gannet went meekly downstairs.

Next day, early in the afternoon, he slipped out of the chandlery. He was monstrously wrapped up against the cold, and bulged all round like a barrel on matchsticks. It was Sunday, and, after the labours of church and a heavy meal, the Gannets dozed and Mrs Jiffy slept over the trimming of a hat. Consequently, nobody heard him go.

First, he went down to the quayside; and then, after making inquiries of an old warehouseman, he went on to the timber yard just beyond Elephant Stairs. Presently, he found what he was looking for: a flight of rickety wooden steps that led up to a crazy, black-painted little wooden house that seemed to be clinging on to the side of a tall warehouse by its fingernails.

As he climbed up, clutching onto a wobbling handrail for support, his legs ached and his breath came short. Already the bitter cold and the strain of trying to stop himself falling over on the icy cobbles had tired him out. At last he reached the half-dozen planks that served for a landing, and knocked on the door.

'Go away!' came a croak from within. 'Dontcher know it's Sund'y? Even the Lord God Almighty had a nap on Sund'y! Come back tomorrer!'

He knocked again and waited, trying not to look down as the ground seemed a long way off. This time the door was opened, and a bleary-eyed old man, wrapped up in a filthy old blanket, peered out.

'Are you Mr Bagley, sir?'

For answer, the old man looked him up and down,

blinked three or four times, then stepped back and beckoned peevishly.

'Come on inside,' he croaked, 'afore you falls off them steps.'

He beckoned again; and obediently Paul followed Mr Bagley into his lonely, perched-up box of a home. Instantly, a stink of old cheese, fish-glue and varnish hit him in the face like a poultice. He could hardly breathe . . .

'Well?' demanded the old man, shutting the door with his elbow and shuffling to heat himself up over a dirty little stove that crouched in a corner, like a stove that had ruined its health by smoking from infancy. 'What do you want? Must be something queer to fetch out a weazen little twig of a lad like you on a freezing Sund'y.'

He sniffed suspiciously, and after wiping his nose on a corner of his blanket, began to clear a space among the litter of tools and wood-shavings on his carpenter's bench.

'Come on, then! Let's see what you've brung me under all them wraps!' He watched curiously as Paul began to unbutton his coat. Suddenly he frowned. 'I see'd you before, ain't I?'

Paul shook his head; and produced, from inside his clothing, a bundle wrapped up in a towel.

'Can you mend it, Mr Bagley?' he whispered, glancing uneasily towards the door, as if he was frightened he'd been followed. 'Please!'

He held out the bundle. Mr Bagley took it and unwrapped it. His eyes widened in surprise when he saw that it was one of the ships he'd made for Mr Gannet's twins. He looked up and stared at Paul.

'You must be the other one, then. Mr G.'s youngest. You must be young Paul!' Paul nodded; and Mr Bagley, wheezing and grunting with pleasure, confided: 'I knew I'd see'd you before! I never forgets a face.'

'But – but I was upstairs all the time when you came –'

'– That's right! That's where I see'd you! Upstairs. Not twenty minutes after you was born. I come up, meaning to put salt in your cradle – which were the proper thing to do – and there you was! all chapel-eyed and mewing like a kitten. Like I told you, I never forgets a face.'

He wagged his frowsy old head happily; then, putting on a pair of thick spectacles that made his eyes enormous, he began to examine the ship. Almost immediately, he stopped and put it down on the bench. His ancient face went stony.

'What have you been up to, young Paul?' he asked quietly, fixing his huge eyes on the sickly, saintly boy in front of him. 'This here ship ain't your'n. It's young Peter's. Where's your brother, young Paul?'

'He – he's away. He's been apprenticed . . .'

Mr Bagley raised his eyebrows. 'Changed 'em over, did you? Done it on the sly, I shouldn't wonder. Eh, young Paul?'

Paul didn't answer. His eyes filled up with water. It was the first time that anybody (except for himself!) had ever accused him of anything. He looked away and stared blindly at a stool that had been left lying on the bench with its legs helplessly in the air.

'Got the worm in it,' explained Mr Bagley, observing the direction of Paul's look. Then he added, softly, 'Like someone else I could mention.'

He returned to examining the ship.

'Can you mend it, sir?'

Mr Bagley shrugged his shoulders. He picked up a tool and, very delicately, began to loosen the seal on the bottle. Presently it came away. He looked at it closely; then he drew out the stopper and sniffed at the neck of the bottle. He frowned and looked up at Paul again; and the black pupils of his bulging eyes seemed to swell and swell, as if he was looking into a great darkness.

'Jealous of him, ain't you, young Paul,' he murmured. 'That's why you done it, didn't you. Jealous of him being the first-born and the better growed ... and maybe because he's the chime-child –'

'The – the chime-child? What's that?'

'Didn't he tell you, then?'

'He never said anything. He just said the ships were presents –'

'– He never told you nothing about 'em?'

'No ... no! But – but I knew ... from the look on his face ... and his eyes ... I knew they were important!'

Mr Bagley stared at him long and hard. The crazy little house creaked, and the stove in the corner gasped and sighed. At last Mr Bagley looked away. He took off his spectacles and rubbed his ancient eyes.

'He ought to have told you, young Paul,' he muttered, deeply troubled. 'You got a right to know. It's best to be prepared for the worst, young Paul, for it's common knowledge that the ship that sets sail expecting only fair weather is the ship that goes down in the first squall.'

He stood up and, clutching his blanket about him, shuffled over to the stove and beckoned to Paul with a jerk of his elbow. As the boy approached, the old ship's carpenter gripped him by the arm and drew him close, so that Paul was almost suffocated by Mr Bagley's cheesy smell.

Although Mr Bagley was an old, old man – maybe as old as a hundred – his carpenter's fingers were still strong enough to keep their clutch of Paul's arm, even if the boy had wanted to escape. So the shabby, wheezing old man, with the thin and staring boy half-folded into his filthy blanket, kept close together; and, as they crouched over the smoky stove, Mr Bagley croaked his weird wisdom into Paul's ear.

He told him about the darker side of the world. He told

him about the mysterious web of meanings that lay beneath such everyday things as a boy's whistling, an old broom, a sudden priest, and the chimes of a clock. He told him about the strange, unlucky circumstances of his and Peter's birth, and Peter's dangerous inheritance ... and the salt that might have saved the pair of them, but had been ignorantly denied.

Then, with anxious looks towards the bench, he told Paul about the ships he'd made, and how, and why, and what they meant.

'If only I'd knowed,' he sighed, 'that his squall was to come up such a howler, I'd have left his vessel under bare poles!'

'But you'll be able to mend it?' whispered Paul, with an anguished look into Mr Bagley's face. The old man's words had found echoes in his heart; and the mending of the ship had become the most important thing in the world.

'Can't say till I takes it out, young Paul,' said the old carpenter. 'You'll have to leave it with me.'

'But it'll be all right?'

'I'll do what I can, young Paul. Maybe after all it weren't the devil's wind what done it, but just me bad workmanship. Could be! There's always a bit of botched work what the eye don't see. Nothing's perfect, young Paul. And just as well. If I was to make something perfect, I'd go and drown meself, because it would mean I could never do no better. No, perfekshun's a dead end, young Paul, it's a real murderer of the soul!'

He let go of Paul's arm and went back to the bench.

'Give it a day or two and I'll bring it into the shop when it's ready.'

'No! Not the shop, please, Mr Bagley! They – they don't know ...'

'So it's still on the sly, is it, young Paul? All right then.

D'you know The Bird's Nest in Jamaica Street?' Paul nodded. 'I'll fetch it there, then.'

'When, Mr Bagley?'

'Frid'y, young Paul. Half after four on Frid'y.'

When he got back to the chandlery, his father and mother and Mrs Jiffy were still asleep. He was profoundly thankful. If they'd seen him, white-faced and sweating, even though he'd come in from the cold, they'd have sent for the doctor at once!

He went upstairs to his bedroom and took out the beaked demon from his chest of drawers. But he didn't put it on. Instead, he stood staring at it, and wondering (not without reason) if he himself was the devil of his brother's inheritance. When he had changed the ships, he had deprived Peter of the warning he might have had!

'Please, please,' he whispered, 'let everything be all right on Friday!'

CHAPTER FOURTEEN

ഢഢഢഢ

'Please, God,' whispered the locksmith's apprentice, worn-out with terror, 'make Friday come quick!'

The phantom stood beside his bed, its face no more than a dreadful sensation inside the deep shadows of its hood; and the air was full of its stink. Then, hearing a step on the stair, it faded away, beckoning, as always, with its empty sleeve.

'You're getting as pale as a ghost, my lad!' said Polly, coming down into the shop, brightly candled and with a bit of cold sausage and a spoonful of pickles for the inner boy. 'Eat up. Got to keep body and soul together!'

When she'd gone, he stared dismally into every corner, and then tried to compose himself for sleep. It was hopeless! Life in Cucumber Alley had become unbearable. The ghost of Thomas Kite was everywhere. If he couldn't see it, he could smell it; and if he couldn't smell it, he walked in terror of its being just behind him, or waiting for him in the next doorway, beckoning, beckoning, with a horrible jerk of its empty sleeve.

Plainly it wanted something from him, but he didn't know what. All he knew for certain was that there was a terrible guiltiness about the phantom, and worse, a sense of ever-mounting desperation. It was as if the dead apprentice had found out that there was little time left to conclude its mysterious business with the chime-child. After Friday, Peter Gannet would be gone from the shop and from Cucumber Alley, and it would be too late.

'And you can say that again!' implored Peter, from the bottom of his heart. 'Please, God, make Friday come quick!'

Jay had mentioned Friday. He'd mentioned it on the Tuesday morning when Gannet had gone for Mr Shoveller's ale.

'Friday,' the staymaker's apprentice had murmured, quite casually, as if Friday was just another day. 'Crane wants the key. Half after eight in The Bedford Head. All right?'

It wasn't all right. In fact, if St Peter himself had come down into Cucumber Alley and asked Gannet for a lend of the key on Friday night, he'd have been just as unlucky. Gannet needed the key himself. He needed it as he'd never needed anything in his life before. It was the key to freedom from the locksmith's shop and its hateful ghost; it was the key to Zanzibar and the China Seas . . .

'But it's for Crane,' repeated Jay, taken aback by young Gannet's hostile silence.

He couldn't understand it. Of all the apprentices in the Alley, the most popular by far was Crane, of Salmon and Kelly's, the wine importers, who, oddly enough, were on Godside and not The Sin. Crane was a pearl among apprentices. Not only was he free with his money (which he always had), but he was unstintingly generous with his master's stock, often watering down customers' orders so that he could better indulge his friends. Jay would have cut off his right arm for Crane, and so would Dawkins.

'You ain't thinking of coming the Thomas Kite with him?' he asked coldly.

Violently, Gannet shook his head.

'Woodcock's coming up!' called out the publican, filling the tankard and, with a deft jerk of his finger, levelling off the overflowing foam. As he did so, Gannet saw, on the wall behind him, the shadow of a jerking arm that seemed to beckon, beckon . . .

He seized the tankard and fled from the public-house, with Jay's contempt twisting into his back like a screwdriver. More than ever, he longed to be rid of Cucumber Alley. 'Please, God,' he begged, 'make Friday come quick!'

At last, God or the devil answered the apprentice's prayer and made it Friday.

There was an anxious, chilly start to the day, and the air was once again busy with snow. Mr Shoveller was late. He came in, steaming and stamping his feet, and complaining that it hardly seemed worth opening up the shop as only fools, madmen, or them driven by need to earn their bread, were likely to be about in such weather.

Immediately Peter thought of Lady Marriner. It was the last Friday in the month, and, according to Lord Marriner, her day for visiting the sick. If the snow was to keep her indoors, the night's business might well be ruined. Frantically, Peter cursed the weather . . .

It was still snowing at eleven o'clock, when he went for the morning ale; and, as Mr Shoveller had prophesied, there was scarcely a soul to be seen in the flustery streets. But the public-house was crowded. Jay and all the others seemed to have been waiting for him. He tried to avoid them. But Jay wasn't having any of that.

'Well, young Gannet?' he inquired confidentially, pushing close and breathing warm beer into Peter's face. 'Or should we be calling you Thomas Kite these days, eh? Just how much are you aiming to screw out of our friend, young Crane, for the key tonight? Don't be shy, young Gannet. Name your price.'

Everybody was watching him. In particular, Crane was nodding and smiling confidently, like the popular swine he was. The locksmith's apprentice felt like crying; but instead, he told Jay to go to hell, waited for his ale, then, with eyes averted, left a world of enemies behind.

On the way back, he wondered miserably if he was doing it all for nothing, and that he might just as well have let Crane have the key. More and more it seemed likely that the soft, innocent, damnable snow would smother his enterprise. Cucumber Alley was deserted. There wasn't even a fool or a madman in sight; only an apprentice, earning his bread. Even so, he walked carefully, for fear of the sudden ghost ...

As he approached the locksmith's shop, the window above Stint's devil opened and Ruby Stint leaned out. Snow speckled her brown hair and glistened on her fat cheeks.

'You poor boy!' she called down. 'Out there in the cold all on your own!'

He hesitated, but didn't answer.

'I heard all about what you did,' she pursued, heaving herself out of the window still further.

'What do you mean?'

'About Crane,' she said, pointing down to the devil and winking. 'You did it for me, didn't you. It was all because of what I said to you. You good, dear boy!'

He stared at her incredulously. She beamed and blinked; and bulged out of the front of Temmick and Stint's like the mockery of a ship's figurehead, sailing blindly through the wild, uncaring snow.

'Best get back inside,' she said, 'or you'll catch your death.'

He stood, shifting from foot to foot and scowling into the weather. Then, as if having made up his mind that it was just – but only just! – the lesser of the two evils, he turned to go back to his iron prison in the locksmith's shop.

Then he saw Lady Marriner. He saw her come out of

the Bible shop. She was muffled up to the eyes. She stared at him; then, with a flash of white silk among her black furs, she whirled away down the Alley like a magpie in the wind.

Instantly, a great weight was lifted from Peter Gannet's spirit. The snow had made no difference: Lady Marriner was out and about. He grinned with enormous relief. Everything was going to be all right after all! He forgot about his misery over Crane and the key; he forgot about Jay's contempt; he forgot, even, about the ghost. His heart was light and his hopes were high as he opened the shop door and stepped across the threshold –

He stopped. He staggered! He clutched at the doorpost for support! He couldn't breathe! He was choking, and he could hear, as if it was somebody else, the dreadful gasping, croaking noise he was making as he tried, with all his might, to draw breath and scream!

He heard Mr Shoveller's tankard fall to the floor. He must have dropped it. But he couldn't think about it. He couldn't think of anything. Suddenly there was nothing left inside him. Everything had gone; and in place of all the hopes and dreams and memories that had once been Peter Gannet, there was only a freezing emptiness and a huge and horrible despair!

The ghost had been waiting for him in the doorway. All unknowingly, he had walked right inside it, and he was suffocating in its stink of seaweed and rotting fish!

At last he managed to break free from its thick and all-pervading substance. He fell on his hands and knees, trembling violently, not so much from fright as from revulsion and disgust at having been actually inside the evil, guilty thing. Although he couldn't see it, he knew it was still in the shop. Its stench was everywhere.

'Go back to hell, Thomas Kite!' he screamed and raged silently. 'Go back to hell where you belong!'

He picked up Mr Shoveller's empty tankard and tottered into the workroom.

'I – I'm sorry I spilled your ale,' he began, when he saw that Mr Shoveller had a visitor. A smooth-faced young man with wide blue eyes was sitting on the bench and negligently swinging his legs.

'Spilled me ale, did you?' said Mr Shoveller, grinning all over his ugly old face. 'Well, no matter, you'd have had to go out again for another one, anyway! It's Hand next Heart, young Gannet! It's pies and beer all round! For here's someone come back to see us, and claim his hand off of the wall!'

The smooth-faced young man nodded and smiled.

'So you're the new apprentice!' he said, holding out a neat and well-washed right hand. 'Pleased to meet you, young Gannet. I'm Thomas Kite.'

CHAPTER FIFTEEN

vvvvvvvvvvv

Mr Shoveller pushed some coins into his hand for pies and beer.

'Now don't go dropping me money like me ale, lad,' he said, firmly closing Peter's limp and bewildered fingers into a fist. 'Make haste now. No need to stand there gawping at Thomas Kite like he was a ghost.'

Peter went. He was so shaken and confused that even his usual stupid grin forsook him. His face felt congealed, like wax. Thomas Kite! Alive and in the workroom! And – and smelling of barber's soap, not fish . . .

Of course he'd made a mistake, a bad mistake; which shouldn't really have surprised him as, according to Mr Velonty, he wasn't capable of getting anything right. But he couldn't understand how it could have happened. He still felt sure that it had been Thomas Kite's hand that the phantom had beaten and flapped at, in its frantic efforts to claim it off the wall. He'd looked at it a thousand times since, and he knew that there was no other hand anywhere near it for him to have made such a wild mistake.

He tramped on through the ever-falling snow, shaking his puzzled head and wondering eerily who, if not Thomas Kite, was the phantom with the empty sleeve. At length he decided that it must be some long-dead workman, still troubled by his ancient crime, whose own hand had long since faded from the workroom wall.

'God rest you, then,' he whispered, remembering with a

shudder the freezing, guilty substance of which the horrible thing was made, 'whoever you are. Only – only for Christ's sake, leave me alone!'

When he got back, Mr Shoveller had the glasses ready, and he and Thomas Kite were laughing and talking over old times.

'Mr Shoveller tells me you're quite a lad, young Gannet!' said Thomas Kite with an approving look at the new apprentice. 'He thinks Mr Woodcock's lucky to have got you!'

'Now don't you go spoiling the lad, Thomas,' said Mr Shoveller uncomfortably; and busied himself with pouring out beer from the jug that Peter had brought. 'I said he's got the makings. I didn't put it any warmer than that.'

'Just as you say, Mr Shoveller,' said Thomas Kite solemnly; and winked and grinned at Gannet, over Mr Shoveller's bent old back.

It gave Peter Gannet quite a turn: not the wink, but finding out that Mr Shoveller actually thought well of him.

'Here's your beer, young Gannet,' said Mr Shoveller gruffly; and young Gannet was oddly moved to see that patches of bright red had come up in the old workman's leathery cheeks.

He took the glass and lifted it to drink, when Mr Shoveller, with a sharp rap of his knuckles on the bench, stopped him. There were things to be done first. Old customs had to be properly observed, for they were the respect a good workman paid to his trade.

'Show the lad, Thomas,' said Mr Shoveller, almost sternly. 'Show him the ways things is done.'

Thomas Kite nodded. He stopped swinging his leg and slid off the bench. Then, with a half-serious, half-smiling look, he walked over to the wall and pressed his hand firmly against the white one under the window.

'Hand next Heart,' he said. 'I claim my hand, Mr Shoveller. I've got the right.'

'Then you're very welcome, Thomas Kite,' responded Mr Shoveller, nodding with satisfaction. 'Now we can drink a health to times gone by.'

He lifted his glass; and the old workman, the last apprentice and the new one solemnly clinked their glasses together and drank to the dignity and respect of the old trade.

As they did so, Peter Gannet remembered the ghosts; and, for a moment, he seemed to hear again the soft laughter and the invisible songs of the weird fellowship of the dead who'd come back in the night to claim their hands. Then, with a sharp pang of distress, he remembered the despairing phantom, beating and flapping at the wall with its empty sleeve . . .

'Not to worry, lad!' said Mr Shoveller, seeing the direction of Peter's look. 'There'll be plenty of room for your hand when your time comes! Over there,' he said, and pointed. 'There's a space for you next to Thomas Kite.'

Then he shuffled over to the door, saying that he was going upstairs to tell the master that there was a visitor in the workroom he'd be glad to see.

As soon as Mr Shoveller had left the room, Thomas Kite, smart as a rat, nipped to the door and shut it. Then he jerked his thumb towards the hanging keys and grinned at Gannet.

'Doing much business with number seventeen these days?'

Gannet didn't answer, which Thomas Kite rightly took as meaning, 'Yes.'

'Let's see what you've got!' he muttered rapidly, and with a crafty look at the door. 'Come on! Quick! Before the old boy gets back!'

Gannet, bewildered by Thomas Kite's urgency,

produced the contents of his pocket. It amounted to four shillings and the golden sovereign that Lord Marriner had given him.

'That'll do!' said Thomas Kite, neatly relieving Peter of his entire fortune, and, in exchange, pressing a key into his hand. 'Made it myself,' he explained, with a quick smile of pride. 'But it's no more use to me now. I'd have let you have it for nothing, Gannet,' he went on, by way of apology as he pocketed Peter's money, 'only I'm a bit short of the ready.'

Peter looked down. Instantly he recognized the key that Thomas Kite had sold him. It was number seventeen. It was another key to the gates of Cucumber Alley!

'For God's sake,' breathed Thomas Kite, with a frantic gesture and a look of alarm, 'put it away, you little idiot! They're coming!'

There was only just time for Peter to stuff the bulky key into his pocket before Mr Shoveller and the master locksmith came in.

Mr Woodcock, dressed to go out and carrying his bag of tools, was in a good mood. In fact, Peter had never seen him in a better; and he couldn't help feeling indignant that it should have been the visit of that crafty twister, Thomas Kite, that had transformed the gloomy locksmith into a locksmith of almost youthful high spirits.

'This is a pleasant surprise, Thomas Kite!' he exclaimed, warmly shaking that smooth-faced young man by the hand. Then he went on to ask after Thomas Kite's mother and how things were prospering up north, and ended up by saying that it was lucky that Thomas Kite had caught him as he was just on his way out, and he'd have been really sorry not to have seen his old apprentice.

'Going out in weather like this, master?' murmured Mr Shoveller, with a shiver. 'It ain't fit for a dog!'

For a moment, Mr Woodcock looked unsettled; then he

laughed and said that a good workman never blamed his tools or excused himself on account of the weather; and anyway, he wasn't so old that a fine fall of snow didn't do his heart good and make him feel like a lad!

Still chuckling, he went to the wall of keys to take what he needed. Anxiously, Peter watched. For a horrible moment, he thought Mr Woodcock was reaching for the key to Bow Street! He held his breath as the locksmith's powerful hand seemed to hover over number a hundred. But it was all right. It was number a hundred and eighty-three that Mr Woodcock wanted.

'Barnard's Inn again, master?' inquired Mr Shoveller, quietly.

Mr Woodcock didn't answer. He looked a little uncomfortable. Then, with a shrug of his shoulders, he put the key in his bag. 'I'll be back late,' he said.

There was an odd silence following the master locksmith's departure, which reminded Peter curiously of other silences in the house. Then Thomas Kite said softly: 'I'd have thought he'd been finished with Barnard's Inn by now. The devil alone knows what they must be getting up to there with their locks and keys!'

'That's enough of that, Thomas!' muttered Mr Shoveller, with a frown. 'We don't talk about outside work. Remember what you've been told. In a locksmith's shop, tongues, like everything else, needs to be locked up.'

Thomas Kite shrugged his shoulders, and Peter remembered that Polly had used the self-same words to him. Once again, he felt that the locksmith's house was a house of secrets, and one of them had something to do with Barnard's Inn and its key. Then the moment passed. Mr Shoveller handed round the pies and poured out the last of the beer; and Polly looked in to gladden her eyes with the sight of Thomas Kite.

'That's what I likes to see!' she said, seeing mouths full

and munching, and nodding her jug-face approvingly. 'Feeding the inner boy!'

Soon afterwards, with a wink at Gannet and a surreptitious dig in his ribs, Thomas Kite took his leave of his old place of employment. He'd got what he'd come for, which had been to claim his hand and get money for the key.

'Now there goes a bright lad!' declared Mr Shoveller, fondly. 'Learned his trade proper, he did!'

Peter Gannet, nervously feeling the Kite-made key in his pocket, hoped so with all his heart.

Although at first he'd been outraged by Thomas Kite's taking all his money, he'd begun to feel that the key almost made up for it. He thought of Crane; and, in particular, he thought of Jay, whose cold looks and contemptuous words had wounded him deeply.

Peter Gannet was a boy who set great score by the good opinion of his friends, and the recent loss of it had been hurtful and hard to bear. But now, thanks to Thomas Kite, everything was going to be all right. It stood to reason. He would be able to regain the esteem of Cucumber Alley without having to give up Bow Street. He could let Crane have one of the keys, and still keep one for himself. It would, he thought with a flash of inspiration, be killing two birds with one stone!

'What are you grinning at, young Gannet?' grunted Mr Shoveller, with all his usual sourness. 'Get on with your work, lad!'

For the rest of the day, Mr Shoveller did what he could to make young Gannet's life a misery, as if to make up for the harm that Thomas Kite might have done by passing on praise. But it was water off young Gannet's back. His head was full of Bow Street and beyond. At times, he could almost smell the China Seas in his nostrils, and feel the Trade Winds blowing through his hair.

Just before half-past four, Mr Shoveller irritably demanded to know what had become of his best polishing-rag. It seemed to have vanished off the face of the earth. Industriously, Gannet started to search for it. Mr Shoveller told him not to waste any more time, but to go and fetch another from Polly in the kitchen.

Gannet did as he was told. On the way back, he went to his cupboard, took out the good ship *Paul*, and wrapped it up carefully in the mysteriously vanished rag. He grinned hugely. He'd thought of everything . . .

As the good ship *Paul* was being wrapped up in one rag, the good ship *Peter* was being unwrapped from another, a singularly ancient and stinking one.

'I done what I could, young Paul,' croaked old Mr Bagley, leaning across the table in the corner of the The Bird's Nest in Jamaica Street. He beckoned to the pallid boy sitting opposite him, and jabbed a mittened finger at the green glass bottle that he'd just set down. 'But there's something wrong in there, something very wrong.'

Paul stared fearfully at the little white ship.

'But – but it looks all right now, Mr Bagley. The sails are back, and I can't see the crack any more.'

The old carpenter shook his filthy head. 'Botched work, young Paul,' he muttered. 'Botched work. A bit o' glue and a lick o' whitening, like the snow, covers up a multitude of sins. But the sins is there just the same.'

Paul didn't say anything; but the old ship's carpenter had no difficulty in divining the direction of the boy's fearful thoughts.

'But maybe it'll hold up, young Paul,' he mumbled comfortingly into his smelly Methuselah of a scarf. 'Maybe time will heal it. I don't say it will; I don't say it won't. All I say is, maybe. But one thing's for sure,' he said, sniffing and blinking uneasily at the little white ship in the green, 'if that there vessel had my name on it, I'd not think of going to sea!'

'But you said it might hold up! You said it might be all right!'

'Might's a frail craft, young Paul. I wouldn't trust much cargo to might.'

Once again, Paul was silent; and once again the old man guessed the troubled thoughts that struggled behind Paul's sickly, angel face.

'You're frightened you done it, ain't you, young Paul! You're frightened it was you that wished it on your brother!'

Paul tried to look away; but he couldn't escape the old man's eyes.

'Well, maybe you did, maybe you didn't,' pursued Mr Bagley, watching Paul intently. 'Or maybe it ain't the wickedness itself, but just the knowledge of it inside you what's frightening you to death?'

'What shall I do – what shall I do?'

'If the sails hold up, maybe she'll ride out the squall. I'm not saying she will, I'm not saying she won't. All I'm saying is, maybe.'

'But if they don't?'

The old man pursed his lips.

'Then it'll take more than you and me,' he muttered, 'to put things right. Even if you run like the wind, young Paul, I'm thinking you'll be too late to save your brother from going down with all hands!'

The gloomy old prophet, having delivered himself of his dark prognostications, wrapped up the ship in the filthy rag and returned it to Paul as tenderly as if it had been a dead child. Paul offered to pay him for the work he'd done; but he wouldn't hear of it. It was unlucky, he said, to take payment for mending his own gift . . .

Paul went back to the chandlery with the ship under his

coat. No sooner had he got inside than he was greeted with a storm of reproaches for having worried everybody to death by going out into the snow. Had he lost his senses? Had he forgotten how delicate he was? Didn't he know that he wasn't like other boys, and that the cold could have killed him stone-dead?

'Look at his poor face!' wailed Mrs Jiffy, wringing her hands in loving despair. 'It's all raw and nearly bleeding from the wind!'

Immediately after supper, he was sent up to bed; and Mrs Jiffy brought him a cup of hot milk with a spoonful of rum, and rubbed strong-smelling ointment into his tender cheeks. When she'd gone, he lay on his back, staring up at the firelight and shadows on the ceiling, trying to unravel the queer shapes that they made. His face was still burning from the effects of having been so badly chilled. Although the ointment had soothed it a little, the pain was still enough to have stopped him from sleeping even if there'd been nothing else to keep him awake.

The ship was on top of the chest of drawers. From time to time, he sat up and peered at it. So far as he could make out, Mr Bagley's work was holding up. The good ship *Peter* seemed to be sailing untroubled through its green world, under topsails as strong as new.

At half-past nine, he heard the family go to bed, and soon afterwards the chandlery was quiet. Outside, the snow muffled all sounds, and Hope Sufferance Wharf was wrapped up in a white silence.

Suddenly, Paul sat up. He'd heard a noise. It was a queer whispering and squeaking, like tiny mice behind the wainscot, or a bird trapped up the chimney. Then he heard a sharp little crack, followed by a softly rattling sigh; then, nothing.

He remained quite still, his heart beating painfully, and trying to persuade himself that the noise had been imaginary and that he hadn't really heard anything at all. But it was no good. He knew it was the ship. He got out of bed and, with a terrible feeling of sickness and dread, went to the chest of drawers.

Inside the green glass bottle, the little white ship lay in ruins. The mainmast itself had snapped and fallen, bringing down the sails and rigging in a tangled heap on the deck. The storm had done for it.

Wretchedly, Paul covered his face with his hands, trying to shut out the sight; and his poor cheeks burned like fire. Then he took away his hands and, as quickly as he could, began to pull on his clothes. But even as he did so, he remembered old Mr Bagley's grim words: 'Even if you run like the wind, you'll be too late . . .'

CHAPTER SIXTEEN

vvvvvvvvvvvv

The snow kept on falling, making ghosts of all the houses and suffocating the streets, until about eleven o'clock, when a bitter north-east wind set in and put a stop to it. It whipped and whistled through the cold white town, worst of all at crossings and round corners, where it drove the fallen snow up into the air again, in sharply stinging flurries that made the running boy cry aloud in pain.

It whirled along Rotherhithe and Tooley Street, and tore the river into freezing tatters under Blackfriars Bridge. It blinded Cheapside, it bewildered the Strand, and it rushed through Cucumber Alley like an invisible mad-woman with a broom, sweeping Godside bare and piling up whiteness against The Sin.

Inside the locksmith's shop, Peter Gannet lay in his bed, listening to the grunting and groaning of the great iron key outside as it swung from its windy gibbet; and straining his ears to catch the faintly winding ribbon of the chimes of midnight.

He was ready. He'd settled up his affairs in the Alley to everyone's satisfaction. He'd let Crane have the extra key, and Jay and Dawkins had shaken him warmly by the hand. In a curious way, he felt that his standing in the esteem of his friends was even higher now than it would have been if he'd let Crane have the key at the first asking.

He smiled, a little ruefully. Then the smile faded from his face and was replaced by a troubled frown as he tried to throw off certain unpleasant feelings of apprehension and melancholy that kept coming over him in waves. These feelings had nothing to do with the business in Bow Street, but were concerned with what had happened earlier in the day, when he'd walked blindly inside the ghost.

The horrible sensations of drowning and despair that he'd experienced seemed to cling to him, almost like the stink of the phantom itself, and made him feel profoundly wretched. It wouldn't have been so bad, he thought, if the phantom had really been Thomas Kite, as he'd always imagined; but Thomas Kite was alive and well, so the dreadful, flapping thing was something mysterious and unknown . . . which was somehow much more frightening. If only he could have seen its face . . .

At last it was midnight. He waited till the last wind-blown chime had died away, then rose noiselessly from his bed. He was fully dressed apart from his boots, which he had left on top of the counter so as not to stumble over them in the dark. His old schoolmaster would have been mightily surprised by such care and foresight on the part of that blockhead, Peter Gannet; but then, Mr Velonty would have been surprised by many of the thoughts and feelings that lurked behind Gannet's stupid grin.

He was grinning now; and with good reason. Providence had blessed his enterprise in the most extraordinary way. For once, the workroom door had been left unlocked. Mr Woodcock had come back from his business in Barnard's Inn soon after seven o'clock in a mood as black as a Bible. He'd flung down his bag of tools as savagely as if they'd been a satchel of school-books, hung number a hundred and eighty-three back on the wall, and banged off upstairs to the bosom of his family and Polly's boiled cod. What-ever had gone wrong in Barnard's Inn had so distressed and aggravated him that it had put everything else out of his mind, and he'd forgotten to lock up the workroom door.

Gannet could hardly contain himself; and, silently blessing his master's misfortune, he slipped inside the workroom as smoothly as oil. He needed three keys: number seventeen for the gates of Cucumber Alley, number a hundred for Bow Street, and pretty little number a hundred and twenty for Lady Marriner's jewel-box.

He knew exactly where they were all hanging, having fixed their positions in his mind's eyes every day for the past week. He could have laid his hands on them in the dark; but he wasn't such a fool as to take unnecessary chances. Unobserved by Mr Shoveller, he'd kept putting more coals on the fire, so that now, when ordinarily it would have been no more than sullen embers, the furnace was burning bright as new. He could even have managed without a candle; but again, he wasn't such a fool as to take any chances. He lit his candle, climbed up on the stool, and carefully took down the three keys, examining each one as he did so. To risk discovery, as every second he was doing, was bad enough; but to risk making a mistake would have been madness ...

Suddenly, he faltered. He stood, swaying slightly, in the midst of Mr Shoveller's redly gleaming iron garden, as if, for a moment, he had forgotten what he was doing. By chance, his gaze had fallen on the pale, flowerlike hands on the opposite wall, and, in particular, on the empty patch against which the phantom had beaten its useless sleeve. He fancied he could see the ghostly imprint of fingers and a palm, buried under the layers of smoke and grime.

'*Who were you?*' he breathed, as, once again, the feeling of black melancholy came over him. '*What was your name?*'

He shook his head. It must have been nearly five minutes

after midnight. Already, Lord Marriner would be waiting for him in Bow Street, with the money in his hand. There was no time to stand and brood over long-dead crimes and forgotten sins. It was the future that mattered to Peter Gannet; the past was beyond remedy . . .

Yet still he hesitated. He couldn't take his eyes off the faded hand on the wall. He bit his lip and, scowling heavily, crept across the workroom, meaning only to satisfy himself that the mysterious hand was really there, and not just a trick of the light. He peered at it closely, and his feeling of melancholy became overwhelmingly strong. On a sudden impulse, he pressed his own hand against the wall.

'You poor devil!' he muttered, obscurely hoping that his action would bring comfort to the nameless, faceless phantom that his own presence in Cucumber Alley had dragged out of the grave. 'Let me – *Ah!*'

The hand on the wall had moved! Exactly as had happened once before, it had answered his pressure, finger for finger, palm for palm! But this time it was much worse. The invisible fingers had begun to twist and turn. He felt them writhing, as if they were trying to twine themselves round his own fingers and hold him to the wall!

With an immense effort, he pulled himself away. He turned – and cried out in terror! The phantom itself was standing behind him! It was staring at him. He could see a faint glimmer of eyes inside the deep shadow of its hood; but they were eyes suspended in nothingness, they were eyes without a face! Then, almost immediately, the apparition faded into the flickering red air, leaving behind in the workroom its customary stink of fish; and something else. It was something that chilled the apprentice to the bone. It was an unmistakable sensation of murder and hate!

Gannet fled from the workroom, his candle tilting wildly and making the shadows heave and fly. Trembling with fright and bewilderment, he leaned up against the counter in the shop, and tried to recover himself.

He'd made a horrible discovery. The phantom was his enemy! It hated him with a weird, invisible hatred against which he could do nothing. Because he didn't know why. He couldn't understand how it was possible that something whose name he didn't know, whose face he'd never seen, should hate him so much! Hastily, and with fingers that wouldn't stop shaking, he pulled on his coat and boots; and, tightly clutching the little ship that was to be his salvation, he went out into the bitter white winds of Cucumber Alley.

All he could think of was getting to Bow Street as quickly as possible. He needed the money more desperately than ever, as his longing to escape from the locksmith's shop had become frantic. He began to run towards the gates; but almost at once he realized the tremendous risk of slipping on the frozen snow and falling over and smashing the precious ship. He slowed down to an agitated, hobbling walk; but such was his feeling of urgency, that it was as much as he could do to stop himself breaking into a run again. He felt that every instant was of the utmost importance, and that the smallest delay would bring disaster. 'Hurry, hurry!' a voice kept shouting inside his head. 'Hurry, before it's too late!'

As he unlocked the gates and went out into the dim white wilderness of Great Earl Street, a sudden gust of wind blew the snow up into a cloud. For a moment, Gannet fancied he saw a shadow move inside the whirling veil of flakes, the shadow of a jerking, beckoning sleeve. Then the snow subsided and there was nothing there. He locked the gates and set off for Bow Street, whispering over and over again to himself, 'Hurry! Hurry, before it's too late!'

while the wind whipped round his ears and brought stinging tears to his eyes.

The biting wind and the sudden, whirled-up flurries of snow were merciless alike to apprentice, man and beast. In particular, they were very disagreeable to Norris Briggs (High-class Market Produce from Kent), who, with his horse and cart and load of frozen cabbages for Covent Garden, blundered about in a lost whiteness, somewhere between Cheapside and Ludgate Hill.

Although both man and beast were wrapped up like a pair of frowsy mattresses, the cold kept getting through, so that it was necessary, every quarter of an hour or so, to top up with strong spirits, in order to keep some warmth within. Consequently, by about ten minutes past midnight, Norris Briggs was, as the saying goes, well away and seeing all manner of strange things; none of which surprised him. He saw St Paul's wobbling like a jelly and the Mansion House sliding sideways, like a huge rice pudding on a tilted plate.

It was, as he confided to his horse, the very devil of a night. In fact, he would go even further, and declare that it was a night of the devil, as, at that very moment, the devil himself appeared to Norris Briggs. It wasn't a very large devil, and, from the look of him, almost dead from running, as he staggered up beside the cart. He might almost have been a boy, an ordinary, human boy; but it was the face that gave him away. It was horribly beaked and grinning, and with black holes for eyes.

'Please, please!' panted the devil, his voice queerly muffled and smoke coming out of his mouth. 'Can you take me to Covent Garden?'

'Hop aboard!' grunted Norris Briggs with a jerk of his thumb. 'On a night like this, you must be homesick for the fires of hell, your poor little devil, you!'

'Hurry, please hurry!' pleaded the devil, as he climbed up among the cabbages. 'Hurry, before it's too late!'

Peter Gannet stood outside number twenty-seven, Bow Street. The house was in darkness. He took out the key and, mounting the steps, opened the door. Quiet as a ghost, he went inside.

CHAPTER SEVENTEEN

vwvwvwvwvw

'I'm glad, so very glad you've come, young man! I was half-afraid that the weather would keep you away.'

Peter started, and nearly dropped the ship. The words, uttered so softly that they scarcely interrupted the deep silence inside the house, seemed to have come out of nowhere. Then he saw Lord Marriner. He was standing bolt-upright in the dark behind the door. He was as still as a stone. It was just possible to make out the faint gleaming of his pale, moist forehead, and, in particular, his hands. He was wearing what looked like white cotton gloves. Uneasily, Peter wondered how long he'd been standing there like that . . .

'Come this way, young man,' breathed Lord Marriner, suddenly stirring into life and beckoning with white fingers that kept opening and folding up like a fan. 'This way . . . this way . . .'

Still beckoning, he led the nervous locksmith's boy across the hall and into the prowling, snarling, silver forest of a room where they'd talked before; and noiselessly shut the door behind them.

The room was full of glints and gleams and glimmers that were reflections of the fire that burned in the grate and a lamp in a misty glass globe that stood on a table beside Lord Marriner's chair. It stared at the locksmith's boy like a large yellow eye . . .

Suddenly Peter became aware that Lord Marriner's

cotton hand was resting lightly on his shoulder, and he felt himself being gently guided towards the fire.

'Sit down, young man,' murmured his lordship, pointing, with his lion-headed stick, to a second, smaller chair that had been drawn up in readiness on the other side of the fire. 'Make yourself comfortable, and – and warm.'

Peter grinned stupidly; and, leaving lumps of dirty melting snow all over the carpet from his boots, made himself as comfortable as was possible for a locksmith's apprentice in the presence of a lord. He perched himself stiffly on the very edge of the chair, with the little ship, still wrapped up in Mr Shoveller's best polishing-rag, clutched fiercely in his lap.

The room was warm, very warm, which must have been the reason for the shiny, sweaty look of his lordship's face as he stood, leaning slightly on his stick, and watching the boy. He was wearing a heavy dressing-gown of dark red velvet, which made his white-gloved hands look as if they belonged to somebody else . . .

'I – I've brought it, your lordship!' began Peter, his voice shrill with eagerness and anxiety. He started to unwrap the ship.

His lordship continued to watch; but he seemed more interested in the boy than in the emerging ship.

'You're trembling, young man!' he observed with concern. 'You're shaking like a leaf! It's the cold, of course! The wind outside must have chilled you right through!'

'It – it's all right, your lordship –'

'– Come, come!' interposed his lordship, waving a white hand. 'You're a frozen boy! Leave the ship till later. You must get warm. I don't want your death on my hands! What would your Mr Woodcock say! He would be very angry with me. And we mustn't make your Mr Woodcock angry. Before we carry on with our business, young man, you must drink a glass of brandy. It will bring the warmth of life back into your poor blood.'

Even while Lord Marriner was speaking, a glass of brandy had appeared in front of the boy, right under his very nose. It was almost like a conjuring trick. Lord Marriner was holding it out . . .

'Drink it down, young man . . . to the very last drop. You must do as I say. I know what is best for you.'

Lord Marriner was standing right over him. He could smell the faint mustiness of the velvet dressing-gown and the warm peppermint that always seemed to be on his lordship's breath.

'Drink up . . . drink up, young man!'

Nervously, Peter Gannet put down the ship on the floor beside him, and took hold of the glass. Although he didn't much care for brandy, having tried it once or twice on the earnest recommendation of Mr Purvis, he didn't want Lord Marriner to think him a stupid little fool. He gave his usual grin, raised the glass to his lips and, with a muttered, 'A long life and a prosperous voyage!' as Mr Purvis always said, swigged down the brandy like a man.

It nearly choked him. It burned his throat like fire and brought tears into his eyes. It went down through his chest like a red-hot poker and rolled around fierily in his belly, from where it seemed to want to come out again, by the quickest and most convenient route.

Lord Marriner was staring at him through a thick mist, and the disembodied yellow eye on the table swam in a sea of tears. Then, amazingly quickly, he got over it. He could see much better and the burning resolved itself into an agreeable warmth. It turned out that his lordship had been right after all. He had indeed known what was best for the boy. In fact, Peter Gannet couldn't remember ever having felt warmer or more comfortable in his life . . . and easier in his mind.

All his uncertainty and uneasiness melted away; and for the first time he was able to see quite clearly that the fears and troubles that had, until a very few moments ago, seemed so enormous, were, in reality, no more than childish trifles. He could have laughed at them. Even his terrible enemy in Cucumber Alley, the malevolent phantom with the empty sleeve, seemed no more frightening than – than the glimmering bronze tiger on the table by the china cabinet, or – or the silver snarl on the lion's head of Lord Marriner's stick . . .

'A prosperous voyage, I believe you said,' murmured his lordship, quietly moving round behind his huge tomb of a chair and resting a hand on the back of it, so that his white fingers looked like terrified mice. 'That's a real sailor's toast if ever I heard one! I expect you were thinking about your ship . . . your beautiful ship that I'm going to buy from you and put in my cabinet! Is that it, eh?'

Peter nodded; and then, in a burst of confidence that showed how much at ease he was feeling, he explained to Lord Marriner all about his passionate desire to go to sea and sail to Zanzibar and the China Seas. He couldn't remember if he'd told Lord Marriner that that was why he wanted twenty pounds, but at all events, his lordship seemed to understand that Zanzibar and the money and Mr Bagley's ship were all mixed up together.

'A long life and a prosperous voyage!' Lord Marriner was saying, and somehow he was standing next to Peter again, and filling his glass from a decanter that had appeared in his hand. 'Come, young man! We must drink to it!'

The second brandy tasted much better than the first; so much so that Peter wondered for a moment if it could have been the same drink. He shook his head. A gentleman like Lord Marriner would never have deceived him. All the same, it was amazing. He'd hardly felt the brandy going down ... which certainly showed you that it was worth getting used to things. He wished he'd started earlier in life; and, with a sentimental smile, he remembered Mr Purvis in the parlour at home, saying that when he was half the twins' age, he was taking his tipple like a man ...

What a good fellow Mr Purvis was! It was a real pity that Mr Purvis couldn't see him now ... indeed, it was a pity that everybody back at Hope Sufferance Wharf couldn't see that lout, that blockhead, that unfeeling lump of wood, Peter Gannet, taking his ease with his good friend, Lord Marriner of Bow Street ... and talking to him like an equal.

He was explaining to his lordship that appearances were deceptive. He was telling him that, although outwardly he, Peter Gannet, was a common locksmith's boy, inside he was quite different. He was distinguished in a very interesting way. He was a chime-child. He saw ghosts and, sooner or later, he hoped to have communication with the devil ...

While Peter talked, Lord Marriner, in his swirling, red velvet dressing-gown, was moving about the winking, glimmering room, like a long dark bloodstain with white hands. It was hard to keep up with him. One moment he was standing right next to Peter, then he was over by the china cabinet, then he was somewhere else altogether. What a restless, perspiring person he was! Where had he got to now? Oh yes, he was examining the ship ...

'Perfect, quite perfect,' he was murmuring. 'I can well imagine that on such a ship a boy could easily sail to Zanzibar –'

'– And the China Seas! And the China Seas!'

'Yes, yes! The China Seas ...'

Somehow the ship had got inside the cabinet, and all the little china figures were excitedly crowding round it, as if it had just come into port after a long voyage, with a cargo of spices, silks and tea ...

As he stared at it, Peter felt a little pang of regret over parting with so beautiful and dream-haunted a piece of work. Then it vanished from his view as Lord Marriner was standing in front of him, so that all he could see was red velvet and a white hand pouring more brandy into his glass ...

'I expect you want your money now, young man.'

Peter grinned.

'The key. You've brought the key to Lady Marriner's jewel-box?'

Hastily, Peter gobbled down his brandy (how good it tasted!), put down the glass and fumbled in his pockets for the key. He found it and held it out –

'No, no! What are you thinking of! You mustn't let it out of your hand. That would be betraying your master's trust. I know all about such things. A locksmith's trust is dearer to him than his life. If his apprentice were to break it, it would be the ruin of him. And we don't want to ruin your Mr Woodcock, young man! I'll bring the box downstairs. Then you can open it for me. See! Here's the bracelet –' (Another conjuring trick, and Stint's bracelet was suddenly glittering in his hand, side by side with the miniature.) 'Take it, take it, boy! And look! The miniature! Exactly the same, just as you said! Ah! That was clumsy, clumsy!'

Somehow, as Peter took the bracelet, the miniature fell to the floor. He couldn't understand how it had happened. Lord Marriner picked it up. The glass was broken. Lord Marriner stared at it and grasped his stick, as if he was going to smash the damaged picture just as he'd smashed the china girl. But he didn't. He put it down on the table, muttering, 'It's only the glass ... it's only the glass. The likeness is still perfect ...'

Peter felt enormously relieved that the pretty lady hadn't been smashed into pieces, and tried to say so –

'– Wait for me here, boy,' said his lordship, with a queer, lopsided look at the apprentice, 'if you want your money. Don't leave this room!'

He picked up the lamp from the table, and, with his stick under his arm, moved redly towards the door. He opened it and stood listening for a moment. The house was very quiet.

'I'll bring the box down,' he breathed. 'She's asleep now. She took a little laudanum before she went to bed. Wait for me here, boy. I'll bring down the box and your money. She won't wake up, I promise you . . .'

The door closed and the only light remaining in the room came from the fire. Gannet began opening and shutting his eyes, in an effort to get them accustomed to the deep gloom. He had a sudden desire to look at his ship again. He stood up; and the room stood up with him, so that he was still sitting down. And breathing very noisily. 'Ssh!' he said.

He was feeling very strange, and believed himself to be feverish. Anxiously he felt his forehead; but couldn't find it. He stared about him wildly, until his gaze fell upon the decanter of brandy, winking in the firelight, on the table by Lord Marriner's chair. With a tremendous effort, he struggled towards it.

'Hair of the dog!' he moaned, dazedly recollecting that Mr Purvis's infallible remedy for drinking too much was to drink a little more. 'Hair of the dog that bit me!'

Unable to find his glass, he drank straight out of the decanter; and lay down for a little while on the floor. Presently he felt better and got up. But it was a bad mistake. Almost at once, he felt sick. In fact, he was going to be sick. There was no doubt about it. But where? He was, after all, in a nobleman's house . . .

A sensation of delicacy overcame him, and he peered round the room for a convenient vase or pot. Then he wondered about the window, but it was heavily curtained and anyway he didn't think he could get there in time. Oh God! he thought, what am I going to do?

He got down on his hands and knees and crawled towards the door. Carefully, he opened it, hoping to find some private place in the hall. He went outside and briefly rested his unhappy head against the blessedly cool tiles . . .

There was a light upstairs, gleaming yellowly through the black bannisters. Lord Marriner was still up there. Any moment now, he'd be coming down. Gannet panicked at the thought of being caught out in the hall instead of where he'd been told to wait. The only thing was to go and explain before it was too late. A clean breast of things. He had to let his lordship know that he'd only come outside because he didn't want to do anything unpleasant on the carpet . . .

Feeling somewhat easier in his mind, he began to crawl up the stairs towards the light, which was sliding sideways out of what must have been her ladyship's room. He reached the half-landing and rested . . .

Something was going on in the room. He could hear it. It was an odd noise, like somebody beating a carpet and grunting each time with the effort. Ugh – thump! Ugh – thump!

He struggled upright and tried to see what was happening; but the door was only open wide enough to admit a view of the wall just inside the room. He saw a shadow on it, a shadow that was moving in a very peculiar way. For a moment, he forgot his sickness and watched the shadow, mightily puzzled.

It was Lord Marriner, all right. But what was he doing? He seemed to be leaning over something and jerking his

arm violently up and down, up and down ... Ugh! –
thump! Ugh – thump!

It was his stick that was making the thumping noise.
He'd got hold of it by the end and was thrashing the lion's
head up and down with tremendous force. Ugh – thump!
Ugh – thump! 'Of course!' thought Gannet, with a sudden
unpleasant recollection of what had happened to the china
girl. 'He's smashing damaged goods!' Ugh – thump! went
the stick. Ugh – thump!

Gannet shrank back. He nearly fell down the stairs.
Frantically, he clutched at the bannisters and made his
way down as fast as he could, hoping to God that the man
upstairs hadn't heard him. He staggered back into the
room where he'd been told to wait, and collapsed in his
chair, shaking all over and breathing heavily.

Although he was no longer capable of thinking properly,
he knew, in a confused kind of way, that he'd seen something he wasn't supposed to see; and that it was something
terrible. He wanted enormously to run away, but it was
too late. He saw the door creep open and the glaring
yellow eye come floating crazily into the room. Lord
Marriner was back.

His face was absolutely drenched with sweat from his
recent exertions, and he'd broken his stick. He was
carrying the pieces of it under his arm. He put the lamp
back on the table and with it, a small, shining box; then he
came very close to Gannet and stood, with his hands
behind his back, and breathing warm peppermint all over
him. He stared hard at the boy; then he noticed the brandy
decanter lying on the floor ...

'Are you still awake, boy?'

Gannet nodded, dully.

'Then give me the key, boy, the key to the box.'

Gannet held it up, and tried to follow it with his eyes as
it waved about in the air. Lord Marriner grasped his hand

to steady it, and took the key. As he did so, Gannet noticed that his lordship seemed to have changed his gloves. Instead of white, he was now wearing red ones. And some of the red had come off on Gannet's wrist, where Lord Marriner had touched him . . .

He'd opened the box; but instead of putting Stint's bracelet inside, he was taking everything out, almost as if he was looking for something . . .

'I expect you're waiting for your money, boy . . .'

Gannet tried to grin; but his face seemed to belong to somebody else, who insisted on putting on an expression of helpless stupidity and terror, over which he, Gannet, had no control . . .

'It was nineteen pounds, wasn't it, boy? Well . . . well, I think this should satisfy your greedy little soul, boy . . . this . . . and this . . . and this!'

With fierce red fingers that pinched and hurt, he was pushing everything out of the box into the drunken apprentice's pockets! Rings, brooches, necklaces, Stint's bracelet and shiny trinkets of every description were being poked and forced into Gannet until his pockets were overflowing with a fortune in Lady Marriner's jewels!

'Now you're a thief, boy, a thief!'

Lord Marriner had got hold of him by the arm and was pulling him across the room. 'What are you, boy?'

'A thief, sir . . .' mumbled Peter Gannet, who was in no state to offer an alternative suggestion.

He was out in the hall, and the front door was open. He was standing on the steps and the cold wind was blasting into his face.

'The key, boy, the key! Don't forget the key! And – and *this*!'

With a final, violent thrust, Lord Marriner forced his broken stick inside the boy's coat so that the silver lion's head was poking out and snarling in his dazed face.

'Now you're a murderer, boy, a murderer! What are you, boy?'

'A – a murderer, sir . . .'

He stared at the lion's head. You could hardly see the silver any more. It was thickly clotted with red, to which were adhering several long, dark hairs.

'Now, go! Go back to – to your ghosts and the devil!'

Suddenly he gave the boy a tremendous push that sent him flying down the steps and sprawling in the snow.

'Thief! Murderer! What are you, boy?'

'Thief . . . murderer . . .' moaned Peter Gannet, crawling away into the freezing night of ghosts and the devil.

CHAPTER EIGHTEEN

vwvwvwvwvw

'I've got to find Cucumber Alley! Please, *please* do you know where it is, Mr Briggs?'

Norris Briggs (High-class Market Produce from Kent) looked back over his shoulder at the queer little beaky demon who was tumbling about among his frozen, high-class cabbages. He thought for a moment, then gave a large, steamy nod.

'Is it far from here, Mr Briggs?'

Norris Briggs reined in his horse and peered forlornly into the blowy nothingness of the wild white night. He scratched his bundled-up head with a mittened finger. He wasn't exactly lost; but he was pretty damn' near it. To the best of his belief, he was somewhere in the Strand; but he couldn't have put his hand on his heart and sworn to it.

Your snow was a great leveller. It made everything look different and the same ... if you know what he meant. Ordinarily, when the streets were their dirty, workaday selves, he knew them like the back of his hand; but when they were all over Sunday whiteness, you couldn't tell one from another. Just like people ...

'If that's Southampton Street,' he shouted, leaning back and raising his voice as the wind gusted up, 'and I ain't swearing that it is, then Cucumber Alley's not above quarter of a mile, straight through!' He pointed to a turning on the right. 'But we'll be going the long way round.'

'Why, why, Mr Briggs?'

'Because if that's Southampton Street, it'll be too steep and slippery for an article of this size and weight. Me horse could never hold it, God bless him! We'd be coming down a sight quicker than we'd be going up . . . and on a night like this a runaway cart would be a horrible murderous thing! Oi! What are you up to, back there?'

'I want to get off, Mr Briggs! I'll run – I'll run!'

'Then mind me cabbages!' bellowed Norris Briggs, as the feeble, undersized demon began struggling and scrabbling over the mountain of green cannonballs, in its desperate hurry to get down from the cart. 'And – and yourself, too,' he added gruffly; for, no matter what it said in the prayer-book, this particular devil was a devil to be pitied, not damned.

There was a real sweetness of nature somewhere inside that hellish, glaring grin. Norris Briggs felt it in his bones. Maybe he wouldn't have noticed if it hadn't been for the face; but the very horror of it, the very wickedness of it, made the sweetness within seem as sharp as pickles . . .

'You want to carry on straight up Southampton Street,' he advised; but before he could finish, the demon was off, limping and hopping across the Strand, black as a flea against the white.

As Norris Briggs strained his eyes to follow the progress of his little devil, he saw it fall over, get up again, wave wildly, and stumble on up the steep hill. Then an almighty gust of wind heaved up the thickly drifted snow at the bottom of Southampton Street like a furious sea. When it subsided, the devil had gone.

'Ships that pass in the night,' grunted Norris Briggs, and, topping up with another dose of spirits to keep out the cold, took up his reins and rolled slowly on, the long way round. Ships that pass in the night . . .

*

There was a ship in Martlet Court, just off Bow Street. Or at least, it looked like one. It was caught up in a sudden whirlwind of snow that was walking about without any feet. But it was never a ship that could have sailed to Zanzibar and the China Seas. It was a pitiful, flimsy thing, like a ship with a broken mast and a wildly flapping sail; a ship that was going down in squall with all hands . . .

Shaking and sobbing, the luckless locksmith's boy, who had crawled into the little court like a frightened animal, watched the weird effect of wind and snow and rags of rubbish that had been snatched up inside it. If only he, too, could have been snatched up out of this horrible Friday night and carried away to the ends of the world!

His drunkenness had, to some extent, been overcome by the cold and the terrible things that had happened to him, so that he knew, in his heart of hearts, that he was done for. Already, he could hear faint shouts and cries coming from the house in Bow Street as it woke up to death. At any moment, people would come and seize him and drag him away . . .

'You are a thief, boy, a thief!' he remembered dully. 'What are you, boy?' A thief. 'You are a murderer, boy, a murderer! What are you, boy?' A murderer . . .

'Thief! Thief! Murderer!' came the shouts from Bow Street. 'The locksmith's boy, the locksmith's boy!'

'No! No!' moaned the locksmith's boy, as he crouched in Martlet Court; but his situation was hopeless. Nothing could save him. Dimly, and in a sick confusion, he understood that Lord Marriner had seen to that. His pockets were stuffed with guilty keys and a fortune in jewels. There was blood on his coat and blood on his hand; and there was blood, thick as strawberries, on the heavy silver top of the broken walking-stick that, only a few minutes before, had killed a woman in her bed. Perhaps he'd really done it, as Lord Marriner had told him. He couldn't remember. He begun to pull the stick out of his coat, to get rid of it . . .

'Thief! Murderer! The locksmith's boy!'

He had to get away! Tilbury! If only he could run and run to Tilbury and get on a ship! He had the money! He could pay a fortune – He struggled to his feet, and the wind, as if outraged by the ruined apprentice, rose to a sudden pitch of fury. All the devils of hell seemed to inhabit it; and every devil seemed to be howling: 'Thief! Murderer! The locksmith's boy!'

Outside, Bow Street was a cloud of flying white, and the whirlwind in Martlet Court went mad. It swirled and danced round all the doorways in the court like a tipsy beggar, with the flapping rags of rubbish still waving and spinning inside. Then it took it into its head to follow the half-blinded apprentice out into Bow Street: spare a penny, mister, spare a penny for a poor devil.

Gannet in the snow, like a little black nightmare lost in the white. He couldn't see Bow Street; and Bow Street, thank God! couldn't see him! He began to stumble towards Long Acre, with a faint awakening of hope. He could no longer hear the shouting voices behind him, and his hope grew stronger with every blundering step: he'd be all right, he'd be all right!

Then he saw the whirlwind, the weird whirlwind from Martlet Court. Somehow it had got in front of him, twisting and spinning and doing mad beggar's tricks: spare a penny, mister, spare a penny for a poor devil . . .

He tried to avoid it. He took a step sideways; and the wind died. Slowly, the flying snow began to settle, and the ghostly houses rose up out of the falling spray and sinking billows like a town rising out of the sea. But Gannet didn't move. The whirlwind had collapsed; but the flapping rags inside it had remained, bolt-upright in his path. It was the phantom, beckoning with its empty sleeve! It stood no more than a couple of yards away, and its hatred seemed to blast the boy right through!

'No! No!' shrieked Gannet, holding up his arms as if to ward off the evil, stinking thing. He staggered back, but even as he did so, he remembered it was towards the house of murder. He was caught between two enemies, one living and one dead. And the worst of it was, he didn't know why they hated him; or which one hated him the most.

He was still holding the broken stick in his hand. God knew why he hadn't thrown it away, but he was still holding it. He hesitated for a moment, then, with a cry of terror and rage, he struck at the ghost with all his strength, again and again and again!

It shrank back. Gannet stumbled after, still hitting at it with the stick. He couldn't stop. Hatred breeds hatred, and the whirlwind had sown a wind as wild as itself. 'That boy,' Mr Velonty had once warned Mr Gannet, after Peter had been driven beyond all endurance, 'has a temper. It must be curbed, or he'll turn out a bad lot.'

The words, the looks, the sensations of that unpleasant occasion suddenly and unaccountably came back to the boy as, gasping and panting, he pursued the hateful phantom, striking at it with all his might. A bad lot . . . a bad lot . . . Every hand was against him, even the sleeve without a hand, even the stinking dead! All he could do was to hit and hit and hit, or be pushed off the end of the world.

Spare a penny, mister, spare a penny for a poor devil . . . The phantom danced and twisted in front of him, now holding out its sleeve, now jerking it back again, like a punished boy, as the stick came flying down. Spare a penny, mister . . . Then off it whirled as Gannet came stumbling, staggering after, with his furious stick.

It was mocking him, he knew it. It was taunting him:

can't catch me – can't catch me! Spare a penny, mister . . . Down came the stick! Can't catch me – can't catch me! Spare a penny – Down came the stick! Can't catch me!

Another corner, another street, then another that suddenly slipped and slithered and tilted madly, out of all possibility or sense. Gannet had fallen over. He lay in the snow, and the shocked houses stared down at him with snow-swollen windows, as if they had white sties in their eyes . . .

Spare a penny, mister . . . The phantom was standing over him, its sleeve outstretched. But this time there was no stick; all the boy's strength had gone. Slowly the sleeve drew back. It was beckoning again, it was beckoning unmistakably for the boy to come inside it!

Peter, weeping with terror and loathing, tried to crawl away. He remembered too well what the phantom was made of; of guilt, emptiness and drowning despair. The horrible thing was bending over him, it was coming closer and closer, and its stink was overpowering!

'Keep away – keep away!' moaned Peter, as the dark, nameless, faceless phantom blotted out the sky. 'What do you want with me? Why do you hate me? What have I ever done to you?' Then, with a feeble flicker of rage against the unfairness of it all, he cried out, 'I've got a right to know!'

The phantom trembled; it shuddered through all its vague substance, as if in sudden remorse and grief. Then, with a queer little sigh, it sank down and covered the boy like a blanket. Then it was no more.

Peter lay very still. All thought and feeling seemed to have congealed within him. He had seen the phantom's face. It had been neither terrible nor malevolent. It had been no more than the haunted, guilt-ridden face of a fourteen-year-old boy. Yet it had shocked him to stone. It had been as if he looked into a mirror. The face he'd seen had been his own!

The phantom that had haunted him had been himself. What he'd taken to be the ghost of the past had been the ghost of the future. It had been his own guilt that had been haunting him, warning him, and now, at the end, *was* him. Peter Gannet was the apprentice who'd lost the right to claim his hand. He was a thief, a murderer, and he'd betrayed his master's trust.

He stood up, aching with self-hatred and despair. Everything had gone rotten inside him; even his longing for the sea was no more than a stink of seaweed and dead fish. He saw the stick lying in the snow at his feet. He bent to pick it up. His arm felt weak from beating at the empty air. Or was it weak from beating something else? Was it weak from beating a woman to death?

He couldn't remember. His mind was in confusion. He could remember going up the stairs. He could remember hearing the noise ... but nothing more. Then he remembered the shadow on the wall! So he hadn't done it!

But who would believe him? Even at the best of times, Peter Gannet's reputation for telling the truth had never stood high. 'You are a liar, boy, a liar! What are you, boy?' 'A liar, sir ...'

He was in Great Earl Street and not very far from the gates of Cucumber Alley. How strange it was that the phantom had led him there! Perhaps it was because of the keys. Yes, that was it. He must put the keys back on the workroom wall. At least he must do that ... for his master's sake, and the trade.

He walked towards the gates. Somebody was there, waiting outside. He thought it might be Crane. He remembered that Crane had gone out with the key that Thomas Kite had made. Maybe it had broken, or wasn't any good?

As he drew near, the figure turned. It wasn't Crane. It wasn't anything from this world. It was a demon, a hideous grinning demon with a savage beak! It glared at him from out of the two black holes, and stretched out its hand. The last of the chime-child's inheritance had fallen due. The devil he'd been promised was waiting to take him by the soul!

CHAPTER NINETEEN

vvvvvvvvvvvv

'Peter!' shrieked out the demon at the gates. 'PE-E-ETER!'

He'd been waiting in the freezing night for God knew how long! A dozen times he'd tried to climb over the locked gates and get inside Cucumber Alley; but each time the cruel spikes on top had frightened him off, presenting to his terrified imagination the spectacle of himself impaled on them, like the small change of the Wages of Sin. He was nearly dead from cold when at last the filthy, frantic ruin of a boy, who had once been his strong, contemptuous brother, came staggering towards him across the snow –

'You're hurt . . .'

'– Keep away – keep away!' moaned the ruin, wildly waving his arms as the demon clutched at him, like a straw clutching at a drowning man. 'Keep away from me!'

The demon shrank back. His brother stank of brandy! He – he was drunk! He was stinking drunk . . . like Mr Purvis on a Saturday night . . . or any other night, for that matter! Suddenly he was filled with a feeble fury over all the pain and fright he'd been through, just because of a crazy, superstitious old man and a stupid, drunken brother!

'It's me – it's me!' shouted the demon, his fury mounting so that he flew at his brother with pummelling fists, as if to punch some sense into him. Peter knocked him down. 'Look ! Look!' he cried, crawling out of range of Peter's threatening boot, and wrenching off the devil mask that had been protecting his painful skin from the bitter scorn of the wind. 'Can't you see? It's me – it's Paul!'

Peter saw. But it made no difference. His look of dull bewilderment remained unchanged. It was as if there was nothing to choose between his brother and the devil; and that the appearing of Paul at the gates of Cucumber Alley was no more remarkable than any other of the weird happenings in his brandy-sodden nightmare.

'Get out of – of my way,' he mumbled, stumbling up to the gates and leaning heavily against them. 'Got to get inside ... got to put the keys back ... quickly ... quickly!'

He looked back fearfully along the street, and then began to fumble in his bulging pockets. 'The keys ... the keys,' he kept muttering, and all the time turning to look back over his shoulder, as if all the devils in hell were after him.

But of course nobody was coming. The muffled street was empty. The white-poulticed houses, like houses with enormous tooth-aches, were still and silent, and nothing was moving save the wind-blown veils of snow. The pursuers were all in the drunkard's mind ...

'The keys! Got to put them back!' he was dragging everything out of his pockets and spilling it all into the snow ... amazing things! rings, brooches, bracelets, necklaces! He was scattering them everywhere –

'Leave them! Don't touch them!' he cried out, almost in a scream, as Paul went to pick them up; and then, in a low, shaking voice, he said, 'There's blood on them ... and there's blood on me.'

He held out his hand. It was trembling violently; and there were long, dark smears across the back of it, like the red fingers of another hand. Paul stared at it in horror; and it was like a nail being driven into his heart. He looked up. Peter's hair was all torn and tangled, like fallen rigging, and his eyes were huge with tears.

'Hand next Heart ...' he mumbled forlornly. 'Hand next Heart ...'

He was sick from more than drunkenness. The worm was in him just as surely as it was in his ship. Old Mr Bagley had been right.

'Oh God!' whispered Paul. '*What have you done? You've* –'

But the rest of his words were lost. A furious gust of wind, finding a hole in the night, rushed howling through Cucumber Alley, hurling up the drifted snow and filling the air with white violence, like smoke ... as if the devil had blown out all his candles at a breath, and made a wish –

Weeping with pain, Paul crouched down and hid his face until the worst was over. When he looked up again, he saw that Peter had found a key and was trying hopelessly to poke it into the lock. He was all snow-blasted through the heavy iron-work of the gates, in white bars and patches, like the ghost of a prison with the grey-faced ghost of a boy inside.

Suddenly Peter's terror of pursuit entered into Paul, and with such overwhelming effect that, in an instant, it seemed that the night was full of pounding feet and the wind was full of shouts!

He flung himself on Peter and began to pull and drag him away from the gates. They had to run away and hide! That was all he could think of: to hide! It was his deepest instinct, and now it consumed him utterly!

There was an archway on the other side of the street, a snow-stifled yawn between two houses. With a sudden access of strength, far beyond his ordinary capability, he succeeded in pulling his brother free of the gate to which he'd been clinging, and, panting and struggling and fighting him every step of the way, dragged him across the street and into the concealment of the archway.

There was a wild flurry of white and, when it had subsided, the brothers had disappeared. Nothing remained to be seen of them but the rising wisps of steam of their frantic breathing as, side by side, they crouched behind a thick buttress of snow . . .

'Keep down! For God's sake –'

'– But the keys . . . I've got to put old Woodcock's keys back before –'

'– Not now! What's happened? Tell me! That blood on your hand –'

'– No time . . . no time! The keys –'

'– What have you done? You – you've killed somebody, haven't you!'

'No – no! It wasn't me! It was him –'

'– Who?'

'Him! Lord Marriner! He said I did it . . . but I didn't . . . I didn't! It was him! I saw him! He did it with his stick! She – she was in her bed . . . I saw him hitting her! He killed his wife –'

'He killed his wife?'

Paul lay still. The cold of the night was as nothing beside the icy chill in his heart as he began to understand the full enormity of what had happened. Sick with fear, he tried to make sense of what Peter was mumbling about; but it was nothing but a nightmare of snarling animals and a smiling lord, of white gloves and red, of a silver stick and a terrible shadow, of a smashed china girl and twenty pounds for a ship . . . Then he remembered the keys again. They seemed to haunt him and worry him more than anything else. He had to put them back on the workroom wall. He tried to stand up –

'Let me go!' he moaned, as Paul caught hold of his arm and dragged him down. 'Let me go!'

'Be quiet! Somebody's coming!'

A figure had appeared in the street, a dark, muffled

figure, hurrying through the night. However, after a moment it became apparent that it was pursuing, not Peter Gannet, but some private concern of its own. There was something unmistakably furtive about the nervously birdlike way in which it stalked rapidly across the snow.

It was Crane, returning from Newman Street. He reached the gates of Cucumber Alley, stopped and peered through, as if to make sure that no outraged master was waiting up for him. Then he produced a key and cautiously inserted it in the lock. As he did so, he looked down. He gave an involuntary whistle of astonishment. He rubbed his eyes and looked again. The vision remained. It was real!

Truly were the unvirtuous rewarded and the sinner set up on high! A gorgeous golden devil smiled up at him, and at his feet lay a fortune in jewels!

He looked up and down the street, as casually as his excitement allowed; then, shaking all over, he knelt down. He picked up the mask and, unable to resist the temptation, put it on and grinned monstrously in all directions. Then, with eager fingers, he began gathering up the jewellery and stuffing it into his pockets.

So intent was he on securing his amazing windfall that he was quite unaware that several other figures had appeared in the street. They were a formidable group of some four or five powerful-looking men carrying sticks and what looked like kitchen implements, such as might have been snatched up in the haste of pursuit.

Silently they moved towards the busy apprentice until they were no more than a few feet away. Then, before the busy one could utter so much as a single cry, they rushed upon him with shouts of, 'Thief! Thief! Murderer!' and seized him with a violence that almost knocked him senseless!

A moment later, Crane, his pockets bulging with Lady

Marriner's property, and his shrieks of terror and denial hopelessly muffled by the grinning carnival mask, was dragged away by Lord Marriner's servants!

'Who was he?' whispered Paul, when the street was empty and the faces that had risen in all the windows to see what was going on had disappeared again.

'Crane ... it was poor old Crane ... But they'll soon find out it wasn't me.. They'll be back and –'

'– We've got to get away!'

'But the keys ... very important ... the keys –'.

'– Quick! Give them to me! I'll put them back! You're too sick!'

'The workroom ... they've got to go back on the wall. There's numbers on them –'

'– I'll do it!'

'It's right through the shop ... there's a door ... it's open. Got to be quiet –'

'– The keys!'

'Here ... here they are. Number seventeen ... and a hundred ... and – and a hundred and twenty ... and – and –'

'– I can read!' interrupted Paul; and, impatiently snatching the muddle of keys from his brother's feeble grasp, he darted from the archway, crossed the street and reached the gates of Cucumber Alley.

The key was still in the lock where the shrieking Crane had left it. Anxiously, Paul glanced up and down the street, then he began to search hurriedly in the trampled snow for anything else that Crane, in the suddenness of his going, might have left behind ... such as a ring, or a brooch, or any other piece of the dead woman's jewellery that would fetch a few pounds.

He needed money. The only hope was for the two of them to get down to the docks, with enough money in their pockets to get on board a ship and – 'Fly away, Peter, fly away, Paul!'

He half-smiled as the old chant from their baby days came, unbidden, into his head. 'Fly away, Peter, fly away, Paul . . .' He found himself muttering it over and over again as he searched in the snow. It was as if it was a magic spell to overcome the pain of freezing fingers and aching bones, and to strengthen a constitution so feeble that the doctor in Rotherhithe had once declared that, while we all, in a manner of speaking, walk in the Valley of the Shadow, that boy is picnicking in it!

But now it was Peter who was the weak one. Paul would have to help and support him for every step of the way. The thought gave him great strength. He seemed to feed upon his brother's weakness like a maggot; and it was more nourishing by far than all the doctor's syrups or Mrs Jiffy's beef broth.

Suddenly his frantic searching was rewarded. He saw something shining in the snow. It was silver. Eagerly he picked it up. It turned out to be the broken half of a walking-stick on which was mounted a heavy silver lion's head. It looked valuable. He pushed it down inside his coat, and, with a brief backward glance to where his brother was hiding, unlocked the gates and slipped into Cucumber Alley.

He could see the locksmith's sign. It was swinging in the wind about half-way down on the right-hand side. Keeping in the shadows, he made his way towards it, with the keys clutched fiercely in his hand.

The keys . . . The drunken apprentice, huddled in the snow like a steaming heap of old clothes, stared uneasily at his empty hand, as if wondering where the keys had gone. 'Seventeen . . .' he mumbled, with a puzzled frown. 'A hundred . . . a hundred and twenty . . . and – and –'

His frown deepened. Something was worrying him. He shut his eyes tightly and tried to picture the keys in his hand. Seventeen . . . a hundred . . . a hundred and twenty . . . and – There had been another key! But where the devil had it come from? Try as he might, he could only remember three keys and the locks they'd opened. The presence of the fourth key in his pocket was as mysterious as the lock to which it belonged. The more he thought about it, the more uncanny it became. It began to twist and turn in his mind's eyes like an iron snake . . .

'Paul!' he whispered, suddenly frightened that the snake would turn out to be deadly. 'Come back, Paul!'

CHAPTER TWENTY

~~~~~~~~~~~

A shadow would have made more noise than Paul Gannet as he slipped inside the locksmith's house. A feather would have been like hobnailed boots beside the lightness of his darting through the dark shop and into the fire-flushed and feverish workroom.

He shut the door. For a moment, he leaned back against it, holding his breath. He could hear a noise. There was a hammer banging somewhere near at hand! A workman, this time of night? No. It was his heart.

He peered round into the redly flickering gloom. Then he saw the wall of keys. Tremendous sight! It was huge and mysterious; row upon row of hanging secrets, gleaming and glinting in the furnace light, like a Bible written in iron ...

He could just make out the empty nails. They were high up and out of reach. But there was a stool ... Up he went, better than a bird. Ah! if only Mrs Jiffy could see her sickly little saint now! deep in crime and murder, and three feet off the ground!

But no time to think of that now! The keys – the keys! Quickly! Seventeen ... a hundred ... and hundred and twenty ... Quicker than a scampering spider, his arms and their shadows darted this way and that, clinking the keys back on their nails.

One key remained. A hundred and eighty-three. Its nail, which was partly obscured by the heavy key hanging next to it, was almost out of reach. But not quite.

He reached towards it, leaning over like a flower bending to the wind. Then, suddenly, he was blasted! There was a key already on the nail. Something was wrong. He jerked back. He swayed. He began to topple. He flung out his arms to save himself . . . and the accursed silver-headed stick he'd shoved inside his coat slipped out and fell to the floor like the Last Judgement!

Shadow, feather, bird and spider fled away, leaving only a boy of ice. A dead boy would have been warmer. And happier. Hideous thoughts rushed through his head. Everything was ruined! All his deftness and new-found strength had been a dream. He was as he'd always been: sickly, frightened and feeble . . . and his brother's destroyer and devil.

The echoes of the disaster had died away. There was silence in the locksmith's house. Was it possible that God had answered the little saint's prayers, and stuffed up the household's ears? He climbed down, and his fear-stiffened joints kept going off like pistol shots. But there was no other sound. Thank you, God. He bent down to pick up the stick . . . and the door opened!

Candlelight blazed in the workroom and the terrible, nightgowned figure of the locksmith stood in the doorway! God had said no.

'GANNET!' shouted Mr Woodcock. Having found no Gannet in the bed behind the counter, he'd naturally supposed that the crouching figure in the workroom was his apprentice, up to no good. Then the full light of his candle fell upon the ghastly, glaring face of Paul!

'Who the devil –' he began, horribly startled; when he saw that the strange boy in the workroom was clutching a murderous-looking stick as if he meant to use it. 'Put that down!' he said sharply. 'Put it down, I say!'

To his relief, for he was a peaceable man, the boy

obeyed. Indeed, now that Mr Woodcock came to look at him more carefully, he could see that the boy was such a feeble, spiritless little wretch that it was a wonder he had enough strength in his arm to hold up such a weighty article, let alone do any damage with it!

'What the devil are you doing in here?'

He took a step inside the workroom and shut the door behind him. Doors were his business; and he had great faith in their power to stop undersized criminals bolting frantically out into the night. Suddenly he noticed that the boy was trying to hide something. He was squirming and fidgeting as if he was full of fleas.

'What have you got there?'

'N-nothing.'

'Give it to me!'

The boy hesitated, then, forlornly, held out his hand. Good God! it was a key that the boy had been trying to hide! Mr Woodcock snatched it from him. He glanced down at it . . .

Paul watched him with frightful intensity. He was thinking that, every second that the master locksmith stood there, Peter was waiting, waiting in the snow; he was thinking of the pursuers, who, at any moment, would be coming back; he was wondering if he would be able to pick up the stick and hit the locksmith on the head hard enough to make his escape; and, most of all, he was thinking how agreeable it would have been if he, Paul Gannet, had never been born . . .

Mr Woodcock was looking at him very queerly. His face had gone quite white. His hands were trembling and he was spilling wax from his candle everywhere.

'Where – where did you get this key?' he muttered, in a very different tone of voice from before; but before Paul could say anything, somebody called from upstairs. It was a woman. She sounded sharp and anxious.

'Mr Woodcock! Mr Woodcock! Samuel! What's going on down there?'

'Nothing!' answered the locksmith instantly; and then, opening the door, he called out reassuringly, 'It's nothing, my dear! Nothing. I'm attending to it! It's nothing, nothing!'

Nothing? His nothing was the very twin of Paul's. There was no mistaking it. The locksmith had something to hide. Paul felt a little stronger as he realized that Mr Woodcock, like himself, was at a disadvantage.

Mr Woodcock shut the door very quietly and came close. His long, heavy face, all pitted and speckled from flying iron sparks, wobbled and quivered with anxiety.

'Where –' he started to say; then nearly dropped his candle in alarm! The workroom leaped, and the iron writing on the wall shook and trembled as if it was going to fall!

There was a knocking on the outer door, a loud and furious banging, as if to shake the house down! The pursuers!

The locksmith stared wildly; then, with a hastily muttered, '*Wait here!*', he snatched up an iron bar from the bench and rushed from the workroom to put a stop to the violence being done to his door.

Wait here! the locksmith had said. An invitation impossible to decline. There was a window, but it was barred. There was a chimney, but there was a fire under it; and the floor, in spite of frantic prayers, refused to open up and swallow the hopelessly scuttling boy –

'For God's sake, what's wrong, what's wrong?'

The locksmith was shouting, angry, bewildered, frightened! He came stumbling in backwards, tripping over his nightgown, with his arms spread out as if to defend his property; and after him, pushing and shoving, came a heavy commotion of men, all wet and weeping with snow, and waving lanterns!

'Where is he? Where is he?'

Shouts and uproar! Faces peering, searching! 'Where is he? Where is he?' Lanterns heaved and swung, and the workroom went mad! Huge black files and rasps and hammers leapt up the walls! The shadows of the hanging keys tore this way and that; and the strange pallid marks of hands on the window wall were thrown up as if in outrage at this monstrous breaking open of the secret heart of the locksmith's house!

'My lord! Lord Marriner!'

The man with the murdered wife!

'For God's sake, my lord, what's wrong?' pleaded the locksmith, his foolish, nightgowned figure pushed and jostled by the searchers, like a frightened soul in the custody of demons. 'What's happened?'

Suddenly there came a cry of triumph. Paul, imperfectly hidden behind the workman's hanging apron, had failed to be mistaken for part of the wall.

'There he is! That's him!'

Before he could move, he was seized by his arms and neck and hair, and dragged out.

'Here he is, m'lord!'

Lord Marriner, bulky, steaming, sweating like a pig, stared at the blotchy-faced twig of a boy in his servant's grasp.

'That's not the one! Where is he, Woodcock? Where is he, damn you?'

'My lord –'

'– But what about my *lady*, Woodcock, eh, eh? What about *my wife*?'

The locksmith flinched as if he'd been struck. He looked away. He looked up at the wall of keys, as if longing for his iron children to do their duty and lock everything up . . .

The women from upstairs had come down. Crowned with spiky curl-papers and flaming uncertainly in the lantern-light, they crowded in the doorway like angels at a bonfire. Mrs Woodcock and her daughter looked pale and bitter, while the maid, her jug-face overflowing with interest and concern, breathed, 'The poor soul, the poor soul!'

'Why don't you ask about *my wife*, Mr Woodcock?' pursued Lord Marriner relentlessly. His voice was loud and harsh, and his fleshy face was bulging everywhere, as if it was going to burst under some intolerable pressure within. 'Why don't you ask if she is in good health?'

'I – I –'

'Then I'll tell you, Mr Woodcock! She's dead, Mr Woodcock, she's dead, dead, DEAD!'

The workroom shuddered, the women gasped.

'Oh my God, oh my God!' whispered the locksmith, staggering and clutching at his nightgown as if he'd received a mortal blow, while the servants drew away from him, as if not wanting to be involved in so bulky and injurious a fall. 'How – how –?'

'– Why, my wife has been murdered!' said Lord Marriner, almost as if he was surprised that Mr Woodcock hadn't guessed. 'And shall I tell you who did it?' he went on, watching the wretched locksmith cling onto his bench to support himself. '*Your own apprentice*, Mr Woodcock! And shall I tell you how? He beat her head in and stole her jewels. He beat it in like a sponge, Mr Woodcock, like a sponge. Your own apprentice. *Your own right hand!*'

There was a terrible silence. The two men stared at each other.

'M'lord!'

It was a servant who spoke. His voice sounded hesitant, as if he felt uncomfortable about intruding on the silence. 'M'lord!'

'What is it, man?'

'Your – your stick. Here's your stick. It was on the floor. I'm afraid it's broken, but –'

He held it out. Instinctively Lord Marriner reached to take it. Then he saw what it was. He gave a weird cry, almost like a hiccup, and his face went as white as milk, as the silver lion, all gorged with his wife's blood, snarled warningly, as if over an interrupted feast!

Blindly, he pushed past his startled servants and the women in the doorway, and, without another word, rushed out into the night.

The servants stared at one another. The one with the stick made as if to put it down on the bench, then changed his mind. It was, after all, a valuable article ... They glanced at the locksmith and his family oddly, almost uneasily; then, with heavy boots and swinging lanterns, they followed their master out of the locksmith's house like a storm departing, leaving wreckage, ruin and bewildered grief behind.

CHAPTER TWENTY-ONE

vvvvvvvvvv

Ruin sat in the workroom, without a face. He crouched on a stool with his head in his hands like a frightened child; while ruin's wife and daughter, torn between fright and pity, looked on.

'It was the boy who did it,' murmured Mrs Woodcock. 'You're not to blame, Samuel . . . nobody can blame you.'

She spoke softly, but there was a bitter reproach in her eyes and a tremble on her lip that betrayed that, in her heart of hearts, she felt otherwise.

'I never liked him,' said her daughter, fiercely clenching her fists; 'right from the very beginning!'

And the maid said, with a gloomy stare, 'They're sure to catch him. The little devil won't get far in a night like this.'

'But why – why?' groaned Mr Woodcock, raising a face that was all crumpled with wretchedness and grief. 'Why did he do it?'

'Money,' said the maid. 'I expect he wanted money. He was always dreaming about running away to sea.'

'The monster!'

'The murderer!'

'The wickedness of it!' whispered the maid. 'I'd never have thought it of him, never in a million years!'

Every hand was against the absent apprentice, every heart was filled with horror and loathing for what he'd done . . . and what he'd brought down upon the locksmith's house. There was no hope for Peter any-where –

'What's that?' said the maid sharply; and she pointed with a finger like a loaded pistol. 'Over there on the floor, just under Mr Shoveller's apron!'

It was Paul. Forgotten but not gone, he lay trembling in a damp and mouse-like obscurity, watching for a chance to crawl away and back to the waiting Peter.

'Who is he?'

'Where's he come from?'

'What's he doing in here?'

Paul held his peace . . . inasmuch as the violent shaking of his limbs and the sick terror that filled him could be described as peace. Even if wild horses were brought in to assist in the inquiry, he wasn't going to open his mouth and give away anything that would lead to Peter!

'He was in here when I came down!' cried the locksmith, suddenly remembering the white-faced little intruder.

'A thief! A thief!'

That was it! He was a thief! Now they could do what they liked with him! They could burn him with red-hot pokers, but they'd never find out he was anything to do with Peter –

'Where did you get this? Answer me, damn you! *Where did you get it?*'

It was the key, the accursed key that had begun the night's disaster! Mr Woodcock was holding it right in front of him. It seemed to twist and turn, like a glinting iron snake about to strike . . . but, thank God! it couldn't speak!

'You got it from – from *her*! It's her key! I know you've been there! You've been with Gannet! *I can see it in your face!*' shouted the key, but in the locksmith's voice; for it was the key that was betraying Peter, not Paul, never Paul!

'Where is he? Where's Gannet – where's Gannet?'

Gannet? Gannet? What was Gannet? A sea-bird living mainly in Scotland, according to Mr Velonty, with a harsh cry and black tips to its wings . . .

'Where is he? Where is he?'

Mr Woodcock had him by the throat and was shaking him out like an old pillow. 'Gannet! Gannet! Where is he hiding?' everybody was shouting, and their staring, glaring faces were shooting all over the workroom as his head jerked backwards and forwards under the locksmith's furious onslaught. But it didn't do any good. After all, why should he know anybody by the name of Gannet?

'Hold on a minute, sir!'

It was the maid. She'd come close and her big face was shining like a pumpkin with a candle inside it. Mr Woodcock stopped shaking the boy.

'What is it, Polly?'

'Why, it's him, sir!' she said wonderingly. 'It's his brother! Can't you see it? Why, it's just like you was looking at Peter through a dirty window! You're Paul, ain't you! You're Paul Gannet!'

It was all over. It wasn't the key that had betrayed Peter, it was, as always, Paul . . . through a dirty window.

'He didn't do it – he didn't do it!' whispered Paul, staring imploringly from angry, accusing face to face. 'It was him. Peter saw him do it. It was Lord Marriner who killed his wife. It was him . . .'

'What a wicked, wicked thing to say!' cried the locksmith's daughter. 'Why should a gentleman like Lord Marriner do such a terrible thing?' She looked at her mother, who shuddered and looked away.

'He did, he did!' cried Paul. 'Peter saw him! He killed her with his stick!' But even as he said it, he knew that his lonely, childish voice was a cry in the wilderness. Nobody believed him; for why indeed should a gentleman like Lord Marriner have murdered his wife?

'You – you must tell us where your brother is,' said Mr Woodcock quietly. 'It's better that we should find him before –'

He broke off. There was a knocking on the outer door. The workroom fell silent. Everyone stared at Paul as if, somehow, it was his monstrous accusation that had brought Lord Marriner back.

'Answer the door, Polly,' muttered Mr Woodcock, turning very pale; and then, 'Quickly, girl!' as the knocking was renewed.

'Maybe they've caught him,' said Mrs Woodcock as Polly left the room; and her daughter said, 'Let's hope so!' when Polly came back with the news that it wasn't Lord Marriner at all. It was Mr Lott from the Propagation next door. He'd been woken up by all the shouting and had come to see what was wrong and if there was anything he could do to help.

'For God's sake, can't he keep his nose out of anything?' cried Mrs Woodcock in great agitation, as if divine justice had made a mistake and it should have been Mr Lott, not Lot's wife, who was turned into a pillar of salt. She seized her daughter by the arm and, with a flurry of dressing-gowns and a flutter of curl-papers, they fled upstairs. A moment later, Mr Lott came in, for, as Mrs Woodcock had rightly surmised, there was no keeping him out.

He was a tall, pale, thin-faced man with a stooping manner, as if he was on the look-out for worms.

'What's wrong, Woodcock?' he cried, before the locksmith could open his mouth. 'The noise! The shouting! I thought I heard Lord Marriner's voice –'

'– It's Lady Marriner, sir,' said Polly, quickly. 'She's dead –'

'Good God! But – but I only saw her this morning! She was in the shop –'

'– She's been murdered, sir, by –'

'She was in the shop, you say? This morning?'

The locksmith sounded startled, as if the news of Lady Marriner's visit to the Bible shop that morning was something extraordinary.

'Yes . . . yes. Didn't you know, man?'

'W-what do you mean? Why should I have known?'

Mr Lott compressed his lips. He glanced at Polly, who shrugged her shoulders and interested herself in something on the wall.

'I'm not a fool, Woodcock,' said Mr Lott, quietly but not unkindly. 'Nor am I blind. I know perfectly well what's been going on. If you didn't know that she was in this morning, then what she left for you is still there.'

'Please, please!' whispered the locksmith, with tears in his eyes. 'No more about it, please!'

'Do you want me to destroy it, or shall I fetch it for you?' murmured Mr Lott, with a lopsided little smile. The locksmith closed his eyes and lowered his head, which Mr Lott took as meaning, fetch it. He left the shop and, a few moments later, returned, carrying a heavy Bible. Mutely, the locksmith held out his hands.

'Revelation,' advised Mr Lott, as Mr Woodcock opened the Bible and began to fumble through the pages. 'I fancy you will find what you are looking for in the Book of Revelation.'

It was a letter that had been hidden inside. It was written on a single sheet of paper and folded once; and when Mr Woodcock opened it, there was a smell of roses in the workroom, faint and a little stale, like a dead summer.

Mr Lott watched with interest; so much so that Mr Woodcock was forced to retreat. He seated himself at the workman's bench; and there, fenced in by the tools of his craft, he put on a pair of spectacles and began to read the letter. But Mr Lott, a man of boundless curiosity, was not so easily defeated. No sooner had Mr Woodcock seated himself, than Mr Lott's thin, pale face rose over the locksmith's shoulder, like the moon in its first quarter, and peered inquisitively down.

Suddenly, he drew in his breath. He reached forward and put his hand on Mr Woodcock's shoulder, for the locksmith had begun to sob and cry.

'Poor soul, poor soul!' he murmured, but whether his pity was for the reader of the letter or the writer of it was hard to say. 'Polly!' he called to the maid who was waiting by the door. 'Fetch some brandy for your master! He has had a great shock!'

Polly hesitated.

'Make haste, girl!'

'Beg pardon, sir, but I was keeping an eye on this lad! If I was to turn me back, he'd be off and back to his murdering brother!'

'It's all right, Polly, it's all right,' said Mr Woodcock, making a great effort to recover himself.

'But, sir —'

'— Do as Mr Lott asked you, girl! At once!'

Unwillingly Polly departed; plainly as reluctant to leave Paul unwatched as she was to leave the workroom with the Book of Revelation opened but unread.

'Paul!' said Mr Woodcock. 'That's your name, isn't it?'

Paul, feeling that no more harm could be done by such an admission, nodded. He was by the door and about to justify Polly's suspicions by creeping out of it and bolting back to Peter.

'You say that Peter was there when it — it happened?'

Again Paul nodded, and Mr Woodcock, feeling Mr Lott's devouring curiosity at his elbow, explained, 'He's my lad's brother. My lad has been blamed. Lord Marriner came here and accused him. This boy has been trying to — Come back, boy! It's all right! I know you told the truth! I know your brother didn't do it!'

Paul, half-way to freedom, stopped. He looked back at the tragic locksmith and the bony man of Bibles beside him. He came back.

'The letter?' he whispered. 'Was it in the letter?'

Mr Woodcock gazed at Paul; or, rather, at Peter through a dirty window. He fancied he saw a bewilderment in his lad's eyes, a pitiful, frightened bewilderment as to why such things should have happened to him. He fancied he saw a bitterness, a bitterness that was painful to see in one so young. It was the bitterness of not knowing why he had been made to suffer for another's sins . . .

'Yes. It was in the letter,' he said, and gave it to Paul to read.

'But he's only a child, Woodcock!' cried Mr Lott, greatly shocked by his neighbour's thoughtless action; for these were grown-up matters, grown-up secrets, grown-up sins. 'A child!'

'He has a right to see it,' muttered Mr Woodcock, who was, Mr Lott often thought, little better than a child himself.

The letter was short and evidently written in haste.

'My dearest,' it began, with a frantic, spidery 'M' that Mr Velonty would not have cared for. 'My dearest! Forgive me! I cannot be with you today! Or perhaps ever again! Something terrible has happened! *He* has found out *everything* about us! For God's sake tell your boy not to come to the house tonight! I'm sure my husband has planned something horrible! I am so frightened! I think he is mad almost to the point of murder! Pray for me, my love! M.'

Although the letter expressed a terrible fear that had, even more terribly, come true, it filled Paul, not with horror, but with an enormous, guilty relief. At last, at last the little serpent of suspicion that he hadn't been able to stop

168

from creeping round his heart shrivelled up and died! Peter hadn't done it – Peter *hadn't* done it!

'You said that Gannet – that Peter saw him?'

The locksmith was suddenly urgent, suddenly fearful.

'Yes, yes! He told me he saw him kill her with his stick!'

'Did – did Lord Marriner know he'd been seen?'

'I don't know. Peter was drunk –'

'– The little fool! Quick, quick! We must find him before Lord Marriner does! If he knows that Gannet saw him, he'll kill the boy!'

'He's hiding, not far from here!'

'I'll come with you! I'll get my coat –'

He rushed from the workroom just as Polly came in, with brandy and a plate of pickles and cold fish. She stared after her frightened master in bewilderment. Then she put down the plate in front of Mr Lott.

'He ought to have something to eat,' she said. 'When you've had a shock, you've got to feed the inner man!'

The archway was empty. Peter had gone. Either he'd staggered away to another hiding-place, or Lord Marriner and his men had caught him. Paul and the locksmith stared at one another in despair.

CHAPTER TWENTY-TWO

The house in Bow Street. Who'd have thought that such a respectable-looking premises, veiled with snow and corseted in with railings, could be hiding such a horrible secret? You'd have thought that the door would have been screaming open and the windows running with blood!

But it was a quiet house. Most likely everybody was still outside, searching the night for the locksmith's boy; which was a thought that afforded considerable relief to the locksmith's boy himself, as, with sliding eyes and slippery boots, he mounted up the front steps –

'You must be mad, boy, mad! What are you, boy?'

'Sick with fright.'

The door, thank God! had been left unlocked. Or was he thanking the wrong person altogether? It was almost as if he was expected ... Noiselessly he advanced into the hall and shut the door behind him. At once the house seemed to enclose him, like a warm mouth with a boy inside it. There was a lingering smell of peppermint in the air; and from somewhere he could hear the faint ticking of a clock ...

'Why the devil aren't you on your way to Zanzibar and the China Seas? There's still time, boy, there's still time! What is there, boy?'

'Time.'

But there wasn't. He could no longer hear the clock. Either it had stopped, or the violent banging of his heart obscured it. He peered up towards the shadowy stairway, half-expecting to see the murdered woman, her shattered head all ghastly, come down to see who'd called. A disagreeable thought. He drew in his breath sharply; and it felt like one of Mr Shoveller's rasps. He shook his head to rid himself of such unnatural ideas, and made his way towards the reddish blade of light that gleamed from under the door of Lord Marriner's room.

'You'll be caught, boy, you'll be caught! What are you thinking of, boy!'

'Paul.'

It was the truth. He couldn't get Paul out of his mind. Wherever he turned inside his head, there was sickly little Paul, done for. They'd got him. It stood to reason. He'd seen the men go rushing into Cucumber Alley; and, after a moment's anguished thought, in which it had become unpleasantly clear to Peter that he'd brought disaster not only upon himself and his master's shop, but on his saintly, harmless brother as well, he'd concluded that there was no future in waiting either for them or Paul to come out again. So he hadn't . . .

He reached the door, and the red knife of light fell across his feet, giving him murderer's boots. He put his hand on the handle and wondered, for a moment, if the dead woman would be sitting in the chair, waiting up for him –

'Run, boy, run for your life! Run, like you always used to run when you'd broken a window or banged on an old woman's door! What's got into you, boy, what's got into you?'

'A ghost.'

He shuddered; and wondered if it really was the stinking phantom with its jerking, empty sleeve that had beckoned him back to the house in Bow Street? Again he shook his head. It wasn't the phantom . . .

He opened the door and crept into the room. To his great relief, the chair in front of the fire was empty. Nobody was waiting up for him.

The coals were still glowing in the grate and the air in the room was still sick with brandy. In addition, there was another, sharper smell, a smoky sensation of burned cloth. It was coming from a nest of blackened fingers that trembled, like the clasp of a lover's farewell, on the hearth. Lord Marriner had been burning his gloves. Even as Peter stared, the last little worm of red perished, and gave up the grey ghost.

He went to the glass-fronted cabinet and peered anxiously inside. Carved out of bone and rigged with hair, old Mr Bagley's mysterious gift still rode safely at anchor in its green glass bottle, like a frail white dream in aspic. Cautiously, he opened the cabinet and took it out. It had his brother's name on it. That was why he had come back . . .

Although he'd never been to sea, except in dreams, he'd learned enough from sailors who'd come through storm and tempest with escapes so narrow that you had to listen to them sideways, to know that many a good man had given his life to save a ship. And was grandly remembered for it. His own vessel was wrecked and past crying over; but the good ship *Paul*, out of Hope Sufferance Wharf, could still be salvaged from the ruins of the night.

He pushed the bottle carefully inside his coat and went back to the door, feeling that his name had just been pencilled in, albeit somewhat faintly, among the glorious. He opened the door. He shrieked! Lord Marriner was standing on the other side, waiting for him!

'What are you doing down here?' softly inquired his terrible lordship, advancing into the room with an almost genial air.

He was wearing a heavy black coat that glistened with

melted snow; and his hands were clasped behind his back, as if he was hiding a surprise.

'You should be upstairs,' he murmured. 'That's where it is. In the bedroom upstairs. Didn't you know, boy, that a murderer must always return to the scene of his crime?'

Gannet recollected that he had indeed heard something to that effect; but did not feel equal, at that moment, to discussing it. Instead, he stood with his back pressed against the cabinet, staring at the monstrous Lord Marriner with mingled terror and hatred.

'But of course you knew it!' said the monster. 'That's why you've come back, isn't it! It's because you *are* a murderer, boy, a murderer.'

He took a pace towards the wretched apprentice and demanded sharply, 'What are you, boy?' Then, receiving no answer, he produced the surprise from behind his back, and, like Mr Velonty with a ruler, pointed it straight at Gannet. 'Murderer,' he said.

He was pointing with his stick, the broken stick with the silver lion on it! It had come back again! Gannet couldn't understand how it had happened! He'd thrown the horrible thing away in the snow, but it had been no good! Nothing he ever did was any good. He was thick, he was stupid! He'd thought he'd come back to the house to save his brother's ship; but all the time it had only been to oblige Lord Marriner!

You're a fool, boy, you're a dull-witted lout! Everybody knows it. You're stupid, boy, do you hear? You're stupid, stupid, stupid! Don't just stand there with your mouth open, catching flies –

Suddenly, rage overwhelmed him, a wild and blinding rage against the great lord who'd tricked and deceived him, who'd so easily twisted him this way and that, and who was now going to destroy him as contemptuously as if he was an unwanted dog, without even the courtesy of telling him why!

'It was you! It was you!' screamed out the ruined locksmith's boy, at the top of his voice. 'You killed her! You! You! You!'

For the first time in his life – and perhaps for the last – Peter Gannet found the strength to accuse Authority for what it had done to him, for all the mean and petty imprisonments he'd suffered, for the harsh destruction of his hopes and dreams, and, most of all, for being turned into a beast of burden for somebody else's crime. He was weeping. Tears were streaming down his filthy face. He couldn't help it. He was sobbing with fury and indignation –

'I saw you do it!' he shrieked, till the windows fairly rattled. 'I was on the stairs! I saw you hitting her with the stick! I saw you! I –'

The man was coming at him! His face was all cheesy and complicated with wriggling little veins, like it had gone bad. He was thrashing at the locksmith's boy, the witness to his crime, with his stick, and grunting heavily with the effort ... Ugh! ... Ugh! ... Ugh!

'I saw you kill her! I saw you kill her!' screeched Gannet; and there was a splintering crash as the madman smashed in the front of the cabinet and filled the air with flying diamonds. Then he went for the china figures, as if the locksmith's boy had marvellously reduced himself in size and was hiding among them! Ugh! ... Ugh! ... Ugh! How they jumped! How they flew! How they burst into a thousand sharp pieces of terror as the silver lion went raging among them!

'I saw you! I saw you!'

Ugh! ... Ugh! ... Ugh!

'I saw you kill her!' howled Gannet, hopping and scrambling among the ruins of the room as the bulky, grunting lord, his huge fleshy face a rose-garden of blood from flying glass and splintered china, came lumbering after, hitting and hitting with his stick, and laying waste to everything in his way. Ugh! ... Ugh! ... Ugh!

He smashed the silver forests, he hurled down the bronze animals, he dashed out the powdery white brains of the blind marble women until the snarling silver lion was no more than an ugly, shapeless lump of metal; while the locksmith's boy, jerking up his arm to ward off the blows – almost as if he was beckoning his pursuer on – fled before him.

Suddenly a silver bolt flew through the air and struck against the wall. The stick was finished; its head had broken off. Instantly Lord Marriner rushed for another weapon; for he was too fastidious a man to soil his ungloved hands with killing. He kept a loaded pistol in the drawer of his desk. He dragged it out. He raised it; but the locksmith's boy was already out of the door, across the hall and half-way into the night.

Gannet was running; that is, if the slipping, sliding, clumsy heaving of his boots through the snow could be described as running. Instinctively he'd turned towards Cucumber Alley, so that he was running uphill and into the wind. As always, he'd made a bad choice. But it was too late to turn back, so he stumbled on, expecting, at any moment, to hear the bellow of the pistol and feel the thudding pain of a bullet in his back.

There were people ahead of him! His choice of direction had turned out to be worse, even, than he'd supposed. Monstrous dark figures were advancing towards him down Bow Street! Men with swinging lanterns and weapons!

His feet struggled on; but his heart stood still. Briefly he wondered if, when his soul fled his body and he died, it would be like the sailors said, and that melancholy history of calamity and bad luck that had been his life would pass before him in review. He hoped not. Once had been enough.

He faltered. He turned to look back. Lord Marriner was rushing towards him. His face in the night looked all silvery and he was grinning with unwholesome eagerness, like the lion. He raised his pistol and took aim –

With a screech of dismay, Gannet jerked sideways. There was a flash and a loud bang. At the same instant, an invisible hand snatched the street from under him, like a tablecloth, and emptied a freezing cloud of crumbs over his head.

He lay still. Somebody was screaming, horribly. Gannet thought it might be himself, fatally wounded. But it wasn't. It was a horse, startled by the pistol shot. There was a noise of harness jingling and rattling . . .

Gannet began to struggle to his feet. Something was grating and pricking inside his coat. It was his brother's ship. He'd smashed it in his fall. In the midst of all his terror, he felt a great sadness. Nothing seemed to matter any more . . .

He stood upright. He thought he could see Mr Woodcock among the men who were coming for him. It was the worst blow of all. He turned back. He couldn't bear to face his master.

Lord Marriner was grasping his pistol by the barrel, turning it into a club to knock Gannet's brains out. Needless labour, as Mr Velonty would have said! He was kicking up the snow, so that it looked like he was wading through a wild white sea.

Gannet swayed . . . and had a weird impression that he'd left a dark stain in the air, as if he'd been leaking shadow. The stain hovered, then moved away, leaving a faint smell of seaweed and fish. It was the phantom, the stinking phantom with Gannet's face!

It was beckoning, like it always did. It was jerking and flapping its empty sleeve with tremendous urgency. But not to the apprentice. It was beckoning to Lord Marriner!

The man must have seen it. He couldn't help but see it! A look of bewilderment crossed his face, a look of bewilderment and indecision. Follow me! the phantom seemed to plead; and, flapping and beating its empty sleeve like a broken wing, it danced and flickered across the street. Follow me . . .

'Look out! Look out, you madman!' came a frantic shout; but it was too late. As Lord Marriner swerved in his onward rush and followed the beckoning ghost out into the road, he was engulfed, trampled and crushed under the pounding hooves and iron-rimmed wheels of Norris Briggs's runaway horse and cart!

'It weren't nobody's fault but his own,' Norris Briggs kept on assuring everybody who'd listen to him, after the dead man had been carried back into his house, and most of the little crowd that had collected in Bow Street had dispersed . . ·. some carrying furtive cabbages under their coats, for there had been an almighty spillage of high-class market produce into the snow. 'He come out of nowhere like all the devils in hell was after him.'

Norris Briggs was severely shaken. It was a nasty thing to have killed a man, even by accident. But if folk would go loosing off pistols in the middle of the night when horses and carts was on slippery hills, then they only had theirselves to blame.

'It weren't nobody's fault but his own,' mumbled Norris Briggs, brushing the snow from a salvaged cabbage as tenderly as if it was a green baby's head.

He nodded and raised a mittened finger to an acquaintance he hadn't thought to see again. It was the frozen mite who'd travelled on his cart. Like the rest of the world, he'd come running to see what a dead man looked like. It was a queer old upside-down night and no mistake: black above and white below, with the snow going up instead of down, with boys running wild what ought to be in bed, and with mad lords killing theirselves off like flies . . .

'I'm sorry . . . I'm sorry . . . I'm sorry, Mr Woodcock,' the other lad was sobbing, sobbing his heart out to a tall gent who'd taken it on himself to look after the lad. 'I'm sorry . . . I'm sorry . . .'

'No fault of your'n, lad,' said Norris Briggs, kindly. 'It weren't nobody's fault but his own. He come out of no-where –'

'It was the ghost! Didn't you see? The ghost was beckoning! He followed the ghost –'

Norris Briggs scratched his head. He sniffed the boy's breath, and nodded shrewdly.

'Them what tipples and can't hold their liquor,' he said, 'sees all manner of 'shtrordinary things!' Then, spying another runaway cabbage, he went to retrieve it, shaking his head and longing for tomorrow and the long journey back to the decency of Nature in Kent.

'Come along, lad,' said Mr Woodcock, laying his hand on his apprentice's trembling shoulder. 'It's time you and I went home,' he said.

CHAPTER TWENTY-THREE

'In our shop,' confided Peter Gannet to his brother Paul, 'we temper the steel for our springs in water, y'know, not in oil or grease, like you might suppose.'

Paul's eyes widened. He looked quite taken aback, as if, at that very moment, oil and grease had been preying on his mind.

'It's all a matter of judgement,' explained Mr Woodcock's apprentice, with a wave of his hand. 'You've got to catch the metal just at the right moment, between the white and the red.'

The brothers Gannet were sitting opposite one another in the back of Mr Purvis's cart, and being rumbled and jolted along Lavender Street, on their way to Greenwich Fair. It was Easter Monday morning, and the April sun, in the article of dazzling yellowness, was put to shame by the daffodil-sellers crowding the street.

'What's that?'

'Where?'

'No. I mean about the white and the red.'

'Why, it's the heat, lad!' said Peter, with a kindly smile. 'You go by the colour of the steel when it's in the fire. Between the white and the red. Old Woodcock's a marvel at judging it. Our Mr Shoveller says he's never seen the like.'

The apprentice was home for the holiday, and Cucumber Alley seemed almost as far away as Zanzibar and the China Seas. He felt quite a stranger in Gannet's ship's chandlery (Everything for the Sailor, but not much for anybody else); and even his old bed seemed unfamiliar and a shade too small.

He gazed out of the cart on the holiday crowds, hastening along to the Fair: a rushing river of bobbing bonnets and flying ribbons with, here and there, an apprentice stopping to buy a bunch of daffodils for his mother or his girl; and getting in everybody's way. He was looking out for Jay and Dawkins and the rest of his friends. 'See you in The Ship on Monday, young Gannet!' Jay had called out after him as he'd set off. 'Don't forget now! We'll have a dish of whitebait together, and a jar of Greenwich ale!' But he couldn't see them, so he turned back and bestowed his attention on Paul.

'Our Mr Shoveller,' he said, 'says he wouldn't be surprised if I turned out the same. Like old Woodcock, I mean. I've got a natural genius, he said.'

This wasn't strictly true. In fact, when Peter came to think about it, Mr Shoveller had expressed himself very differently indeed. Nevertheless, Peter couldn't see any harm in representing opinions as being more favourable than, in the heat of an unlucky moment, they'd actually been. After all, it was like Jay said when everybody kept quiet about what had really happened on that terrible Friday night that now seemed so long ago: 'There's no sense in shouting the truth from the house-tops, young Gannet, if it's going to bring the houses tumbling down!'

He was right. You'd have thought the world would have come to an end after everything that had happened; but it hadn't. The house in Bow Street was quietly shut up; and, early one rainy morning, Lord and Lady Marriner, with the assistance of four glossy horses and several discreet persons in black, removed themselves to a more retired situation underground, where, in the stonemason's dignified words, they were 'Together in God'. There was no mention of a jealous husband murdering his wife because he'd found out about her love-affair with a locksmith from Cucumber Alley. There wasn't enough room.

It was the same in the locksmith's shop, where you'd have thought, at the very least, the roof would have fallen in; but the Woodcocks still sat down to a family table, ate family dinners and talked family talk — except, of course, when Polly came into the room. And even when Mr Woodcock, poor soul! brought himself at last to take down number a hundred and eighty-three from the wall of keys and put it in his bag of tools, Mr Shoveller only said, 'Barnard's Inn, master?' and Mr Woodcock replied, very calm and quiet, 'That's right, Mr Shoveller, Barnard's Inn. Just one or two things left to clear up, you know. Just — just finishing up, you understand.'

Not a word was said about the door the key opened, the door to that secret place in Barnard's Inn where the locksmith and his love used to meet, on the last Friday of every month.

'They're worse than us,' said Jay to young Gannet, who was truly shocked to find out that the respectable, grown-up world was as sinful and dishonest as himself. 'You'd be surprised if you knew what went on in the Alley, on Godside just as much as The Sin. But then like I told you before, there ain't no sense in shouting the truth from the house-tops, if it's going to bring the houses tumbling down!'

It was, thought Gannet, a shabby old world, but, no doubt, things would be brighter and better in Zanzibar and the China Seas . . .

Half Greenwich Fair seemed to have squeezed itself inside The Ship, men, women, children and even tipsy-looking babes in arms, all laughing and talking and eating and drinking without a thought of sinking any fathoms deeper than the floor. For The Ship was a ship that sailed nowhere, save in a drunkard's dreams. It was a weather-boarded old box of a public-house that gazed out over the river with bulging, bottle-glass eyes.

'A long life and a prosperous voyage!' cried Mr Purvis, clinking his rum with the brothers' ale; for Mr Purvis, red-faced, overflowing Mr Purvis, no matter what he himself had beneficially imbibed at his mother's knee, was on his sacred honour not to indulge the boys in his charge with anything strong.

'A long life and a prosperous voyage!' echoed the Gannets, disappearing into their tankards, up to their eyes.

They were sitting in a window-bay; and Peter was dividing his attention between looking out for his friends in the crowded parlour, and watching the wide, busy river that flashed and glinted in the sun. A ship was sailing upstream, a lazy ship under weary topsails, for there wasn't much wind. It was low in the water, as if it was heavily laden with silks and spices, bright parrots and maybe a monkey or two. It looked strangely dreamlike as it wobbled by, through the rippled, greenish glass. Peter sighed; and, for a moment, Paul thought there were tears in his brother's eyes . . .

'Gannet! Gannet! Young Gannet!' came a sudden, eager shout.

Together, the brothers turned. They couldn't help it as they both answered to the same name.

Jay had arrived at last, good old sturdy Jay! He was shouting and waving and pushing his way through the crowd with a radiant grin that was almost too big for his face.

'Gannet! Gannet! Here we are! You can order the

whitebait! Crane's got the money and he's going to pay!'

The crowd divided like the waters of the Red Sea, as the apprentices of Cucumber Alley came roaring in!

They'd got a girl with them. Or they might have had. It wasn't easy to see. Daffodils! They'd been buying her daffodils! Hundreds and hundreds of them! They must have spent a fortune! All you could see was an explosion of yellow trumpets with a pair of soft brown eyes peeping out, like bumble-bees drunk with nectar.

'It's me, Peter Gannet, it's me,' said the trumpets. They parted, and there, like a silent fanfare, stood Ruby Stint!

But what a Ruby Stint! Slender, almost, as the stems of the flowers that she clutched, she blushed and blossomed under the heart-warming beams of universal admiration!

'Stays,' murmured Jay to the awe-struck Peter. 'Made 'em for her meself. Not bad, don't you think?'

With humble wire and whalebone, he'd given Ruby's opulence a form, and her wide invention a shape. There was a smile on his face as he gazed on his handiwork; it was a smile that Peter had seen before. He'd seen it on the face of Mr Shoveller, and Mr Woodcock, and even on the face of Thomas Kite when he'd handed over the key (now alas! confiscated) that he'd made himself. It was the deep and abiding smile of a craftsman for a piece of work well done.

Whitebait was ordered; The Ship was famous for them. Indeed, it was said that the whitebait themselves, once they knew they were for The Ship, went proudly into the frying-pan, and died with self-respect.

The whitebait arrived with jars of Greenwich ale; and the apprentices came clustering round, with Ruby in their midst. The air was full of the smell of fish, but there wasn't a ghost in sight.

'Peter,' murmured Paul, awkwardly.

'What is it?'

'Now that I'm helping in the shop, Pa pays me every week.'

'About time, too.'

'I could let you have the money, Peter ...'

'What for?'

'For – for Zanzibar and the China Seas.'

Peter stared at him; and Paul, deep-thinking though he was, found his brother's look hard to divine. Peter looked away. He stared out of the window. The ship, with its cargo of silks and spices and parrots and monkeys, had sailed out of view.

'Better keep the money for yourself, Paul,' he said. 'Maybe you'll want to go to Zanzibar and the China Seas.'

'And – and you?'

'Oh, I'd sooner make wonders than waste time going to see them,' he said. 'Like my friend Jay.'

It was summertime in Cucumber Alley, and not a cucumber in sight. But then the name, like the grin on the face of Stint's devil, or the hope in Hope Sufferance Wharf, was only a remembrance of old times, and not an attempt to deceive.

It was six o'clock in the morning, and the locksmith's boy was at work, as quietly as he could. But he wasn't quiet enough. Up shot the window of Temmick and Stint's, and out came the head of the jeweller's daughter. She'd heard a noise, and fear had clutched at her heart. She looked down, and there he was: the locksmith's boy, standing on the iron ring and oiling the hinges on the devil's neck.

'It's for that key again, isn't it!' she said bitterly, thinking of all she stood to lose.

'That's right,' said Peter Gannet, who, like Thomas

Kite before him, had laboured long and secretly to make another key for the gates.

'And I thought you were my friend,' said Ruby, feeling like bursting into tears.

'Right again,' said Peter, climbing down and wiping his hands on one of Mr Shoveller's rags. 'I am.'

'Then why are you lending out the key again? Answer me that!'

'I want to get rid of my rivals,' he said. 'I want to keep you all for myself!'

Ruby pondered; and then, when she'd worked it out in her head, she smiled like the summer's sun. 'That's clever!' she said.

Peter Gannet grinned. He felt like a king. Nobody had ever called him clever before. If only Mr Velonty could have heard!